Culture and Gender of Voice Pitch

Culture and Gender of Voice Pitch
A Sociophonetic Comparison of the Japanese and Americans

Ikuko Patricia Yuasa

Published by Equinox Publishing Ltd.

UK: 1 Chelsea Manor Studios, Flood Street, London SW3 5SR
USA: DBBC, 28 Main Street, Oakville, CT 06779

www.equinoxpub.com

First published 2008. This paperback edition published 2010.

British Library Cataloguing-in-Publication Data

A catalogue record for this book is available from the British Library.

ISBN-13   978 1 84553 906 1   (paperback)

Library of Congress Cataloging-in-Publication Data

Yuasa, Ikuko Patricia.
    Culture and gender of voice pitch : a sociophonetic comparison of the Japanese and Americans / Ikuko Patricia Yuasa.
       p. cm.
    Includes bibliographical references and index.
    ISBN 978-1-84553-350-2 (hb)
    1. Voice. 2. Language and culture. 3. Phonetics. 4. Language and languages—Sex differences. 5. Japanese language—Social aspects. 6. English language—United States—Social aspects. I. Title.
    P235.5.Y83   2008
    414'.6—dc22
                        2007045842

Typeset by S.J.I. Services, New Delhi
Printed and bound in Great Britain by Lightning Source, Milton Keynes, UK

For Naomi

Contents

List of Figures

List of Tables

Acknowledgments

I wish to express special gratitude to Dr Yoko Hasegawa at the University of California, Berkeley, who contributed generous amounts of time and provided excellent guidance and recommendations towards the contents of most chapters of this volume. My research was also greatly facilitated by numerous thought-provoking conversations which I held with Dr Robin Lakoff at the University of California, Berkeley. Further, I am grateful to Dr John Ohala for his valuable suggestions on technical matters in acoustic phonetics and the use of the software at the Phonology Lab., University of California, Berkeley.

Notes on transcription of Japanese

Phonemic transcription of the *kunree*-style romanization was adopted for Japanese terms and example sentences in the Japanese language. For proper nouns, author names, titles of books and articles, and publishers' names, I utilized the Hepburn-style romanization system. In the *kunree*-style, long vowels are expressed as double vowels (for example, */ookii/* rather than */oki/* ('big')). Examples of some other differences between the two romanization systems are as follow (the first component in each pair is in the *kunree* system, and the second in the Hepburn system): *hu/fu, ti/chi, tu/tsu, si/shi, zi/ji, sya/sha, tya/cha, zya/ja,* and so on.

Introduction

The major task of the book is a sociophonetic exploration of voice pitch characteristics of men and women across the differing cultures (nations) of Japan and America. Prosodic features such as voice pitch are an unconscious yet socially and culturally constructed linguistic property. While voice pitch can be roughly determined by the anatomical differences of individuals, it can also at the same time be an excellent linguistic resource which carries social meanings (such as gender identity and other socially salient categories). Thus, this volume argues for the socio-cultural implications of the role of voice pitch in two universal human behaviors: the expression of emotion and politeness. Both of these human behaviors are found to be critical in the understanding of voice pitch modulation of conversational speech across cultures of Japan and Americas. I tender acoustic phonetic evidence as well as discourse analyses in support of the aforementioned human behavioral concepts in construing an individual's voice pitch modulation as utilized in conversational speech. Chapters 4 and 5 of this volume, therefore, contain sections examining the complexities of these notions of emotion and politeness as they relate to cultural similarities and differences of both societies in the socio-cultural investigations of voice pitch.

Pitch

Pitch is the prosodic feature with which this book is concerned. According to Crystal (1971: 200), prosodic features are 'meaningful contrasts due to variations in the attributes of pitch, loudness, and duration'. Crystal notes that these attributes do not have an identifying relationship to physical measurements of vocal cord vibrations or speed of articulation. Nevertheless, they are primarily related to these measurements. I acknowledge that the prosodic features other than pitch as well as a combination of these attributes can be important for sociocultural understanding of voice usage. This book, however, focuses on pitch as a sociocultural phenomenon and thus the effects of other features will neither be included nor incorporated into my analyses and conclusions.

Pitch is also one of the variations in tone of voice, the phenomena denoted as 'paralanguage' (Crystal, 1997: 277). The term 'paralanguage' was first used by A. A. Hill, but it only came into common use through the efforts of Trager in 1958 (Trager, 1958: 8) divided paralanguage into 'voice set', 'voice qualities', and 'vocalizations'. 'Pitch range,' which was considered as one of the 'voice qualities,' was identified specifically as 'spread upward or downward, or narrowed from above or below' in voice pitch. The patterns of such pitch-movements that occur in the language are referred to as the intonation (Crystal, 1971: 200). Crystal (1997: 277) remarks that paralanguage, particularly intonation, is less systematic than prosodic features.

Paralanguage has also been conceived of being part and parcel of metalanguage. According to Trager (1958: 8), paralanguage was formerly referred to as 'metalinguistic phonology' and thus should be regarded as part of metalinguistic area of activity in communication systems. He writes:

> The full statement of the point-by-point and pattern-by-pattern
> relations between language and any of the other cultural systems
> will contain all the 'meaning' of the linguistic forms, and will
> constitute the metalinguisics of that culture. (Trager, 1949: 7)

For Crystal (1997: 239), metalanguage is an 'overall relation of the linguistic system to the other systems of behavior in the associated culture'. Therefore, paralinguistic features signal attitude, social role or some other language-specific meaning (Crystal, 1997: 277). Crystal argues that some values of these prosodic features permanently characterize speakers' speech according to their social roles (Crystal, 1971: 200). He divides the function of prosodic features into five generally recognized categories of sex, age, status, occupation and speech functions (genres) (Crystal, 1971: 188).

Pitch is also an auditory property which relates to the listener's judgments as to whether a sound is high or low. For speech sounds which produce complex, periodic sound waves, the pitch is referred to as the fundamental frequency or F0. Each opening and closing of the vocal cords causes a peak of air pressure, creating a sound wave. When sound waves reach the eardrum, they cause it to vibrate such that we perceive that sound. The pitch of a sound, thus, depends on the original vibration of the vocal cords (Ladefoged, 1982: 168). The more quickly the vocal cords vibrate, the higher the pitch: a sound perceived as a high pitch contains a higher frequency of vibration than a sound perceived as a low pitch. For speech sounds which produce complex, periodic sound waves, the pitch is referred to as the fundamental frequency. The pitch of a speaker's voice thus normally coincides with fundamental frequency. In short, pitch is a subjective perception of a stimulus. The following figure demonstrates the complex, periodic sound waves of the vowel [e] as in the Japanese discourse filler *ee* ('well') being repeated:

The ability for human ears to estimate exact differences in the width of pitch movements which various speakers employ is limited. Thus, the only task which human ears could perform is to decide whether one width of a pitch movement is larger than the other or ascertain if there is a general (relative) difference in pitch movements between speakers or groups of speakers. The motivation for my investigation of voice pitch modulation sprang from my impressionistic observation that speakers of Japanese seem to adopt different pitch fluctuations according to with whom they converse. More precisely, they seem to widen pitch movements more often when they speak with someone with whom they are already familiar, compared with when they communicate with those who are unfamiliar. In order to investigate this impressionistically perceived phenomenon, the actual width of pitch modulation employed

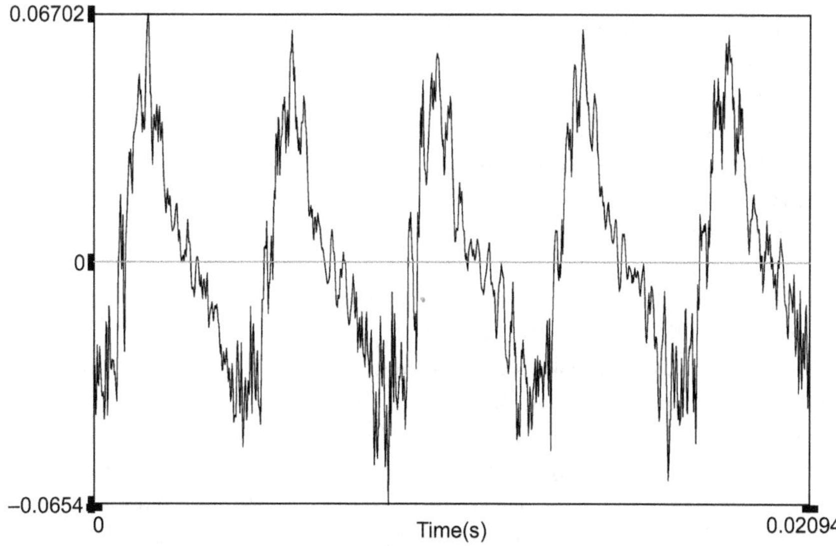

Figure 0.1 The complex waveform produced when the author pronounced the vowel [e] in the Japanese discourse filler *ee* ('well').

in these different situations need to be instrumentally measured. That is, I employed the instrumental approach to pitch examination.

Since pitch is a subjective perception of a stimulus, it cannot be measured directly (Moore, 1997: 3). However, acoustic phonetics – the study of physical properties of speech sound – makes pitch measurement possible through indirect instrumental techniques. As mentioned above, the pitch of a speaker's voice adequately corresponds to fundamental frequency. It can, thus, be estimated by calculating frequency of vibration, the number of complete cycles of vocal cords' vibrations per second. The unit used for measuring frequency is Hertz (Hz). Throughout the course of discussion in the following chapters pitch will often be expressed as fundamental frequency, or F0, indicating that it is an acoustically measured entity.

The present volume focuses on voice pitch modulation, pitch range, that is, how high and low our voice rises and falls. Pitch rise is achieved mainly by contractions of the CT (cricothyroid) muscle which stretch the vocal cords with a consequent decrease in the mass and increase in the stiffness of the vocal cords in the larynx (Hirose, 1997: 133–4). An increase in airflow from the lungs, which involve the entire respiratory system, also contributes to the pitch rise. Similarly, decrease in the activity of the CT muscle lowers pitch and so does the reduction in the air supply from the lungs. Readers who may be interested in visual presentations of the location of the human vocal cords and the positions of cricoid and thyroid cartilages in the larynx, will find them in Rossing's figures (1982: 282).

Contractions of the CT (cricothyroid) muscle (connected to the vocal cords) as well as increases in airflow from the lungs accomplish pitch rise. The increase in subglottal air pressure means that the entire respiratory system is involved in pitch rise. A very small rise in pitch requires very little contraction of the CT muscle and airflow from the lungs. Two basic pitch movements, characterized as rising and falling, create numerous combinations of intonation contour. Throughout the chapters of this volume, the term, 'intonation' in addition to 'pitch' appears frequently. English is a stress-accented language and Japanese a pitch-accented one. In English, pitch is the strongest cue in determining whether or not a syllable is stressed (Fry, 1958). The semantically important words of an English sentence tend to receive stress with high pitch (Pike, 1945: 118), consequently creating intonation patterns. Japanese is said to be a word pitch language in which the relative difference of pitch is fixed in each word. In actual speech intonation, nevertheless, the occasional high pitch is placed at the higher part of a word due to emphasis on any word of a Japanese sentence without distorting an inherent pitch pattern of any Japanese word (Jimbo, 1925: 666). In fact, Japanese word pitch and intonation sometimes do overlap or clash; but each retains its own foundation as a general rule (Abe, 1955: 338). In addition, striking similarities in intonation curves are observed in English and Japanese (Abe, 1955: 346). This difference between the two languages' accent characteristics, therefore, does not create an obstacle in comparing the voice pitch modulation of both languages.

Physical differences between male and female larynges and voice pitch

Differences between male and female larynges appear to have been first documented in the late nineteenth century. This includes Beclard's (554–65) entry in a medical encyclopedia[1] and research conducted in Germany by Taguchi (1889: 5–6). The differences were summarized by Ellis in his 1929 book *Man and Woman*. As Ellis makes clear, the larynx of a typical woman is positioned higher in the neck then that of a man. It is also approximately one-third smaller. However, the transverse diameter shows relatively little difference across sexes. Nevertheless, the anterior-posterior diameter exhibits considerable difference. The vocal chords of men are significantly longer than those of women, with most of the extra growth occurring between the ages 14 and 30. Male vocal chords grow from 13 mm to 30 mm while female vocal cords grow from 12 mm to only 20 mm (Ellis, 1929: 103).

Additional differences between male and female larynges have continued to be discovered. In 1983 Titze drew a comparison between male and female larynges in terms of overall size, vocal fold membranous length, elastic properties of tissue, prephonatory glottal shape based on data from other investigations and some new results from computer synthesis. He confirmed that fundamental frequency is inversely related to the membranous length of the vocal folds. That is, males have longer vocal folds than females, and decreasing frequency is related to increasing length of vocal folds in the scale factor of 1.6. The conclusion was derived from the previous studies, which include a finding that a male membranous vocal fold length is approximately 60 percent longer than that of the female (Kahane, 1978; Hirano 1983; Titze, 1989: 1699)

Titze, however, came to the conclusion that differences in thickness of the vocal folds do not account for male-female differences in fundamental frequency. This observation is in conflict with the finding of

Hollien's 1960 study, which discovered that males have thicker vocal folds than females, and that increasing frequency is related to decreasing thickness of vocal folds. According to Titze, during adolescence male vocal folds do not grow disproportionately in thickness, but only in membranous length. As tissue mass is added to vocal folds, stiffness is added at the same time because the tissue is attached to the boundaries and does not dangle freely. Moreover, the fundamental frequency depends solely on the ratio of the stiffness to tissue mass, rather than on the stiffness itself. Therefore, increased thickness of vocal folds would not cause any change in F0. In addition, thickness and length of vocal folds appear to be inversely proportional. As Titze points out (Titze, 1989: 1702), the longer the vocal folds are, the thinner they are in width. Titze emphasizes that the vocal fold length accounts almost entirely for sex differences in average F0, mean airflow (from the lungs), and aerodynamic power (the mean subglottal pressure multiplied by the mean airflow) produced during the phonation of the voice (Titze, 1989: 1706). The results of Sulter, Schutte and Miller, nevertheless, are in agreement with Hollien's measurements (Sulter *et al.*, Schutte and Miller, 1996: 185).

In 1983 Graddol and Swann reviewed some work that explored the interaction between physical, social and linguistic influences on speaking fundamental frequency space and conducted additional research re-examining this relationship. They argue that a speaker's limits in his/her ability to control the fundamental frequency of voice due to physical characteristics of their larynx may not in reality be the main determining factors of the fundamental frequency range used in normal speaking (Graddol and Swann, 1983: 353).

It is generally believed that there is some association between overall body build and vocal fold/vocal tract size, and thus also between fundamental speaking frequency and body/vocal organ size. However, when examining empirical studies of the relationship between body build and fundamental frequency of speaking voice (by such researchers as Lass and Brown, 1978; Majewski, Hollien and Zalewski, 1972), Graddol and Swann found no statistically significant correlation between height, weight and measures such as body surface area, and mean fundamental speaking frequency (Graddol and Swann, 1983: 353).

Graddol and Swann also discuss several studies in which listeners could not demonstrate their ability to make accurate estimates of speakers' physical characteristics by listening to the voices of informants (e.g., Lass *et al.*, 1979; 1980 cited in Graddol and Swann, 1983; Gunter and Manning, 1982). This was shown to hold true across a variety of speech conditions as well as a variety of methods of estimating height and weight, including speech consisting of filtered first formant and filtered second formant (Graddol and Swann, 1983: 353). Graddol and Swann concluded that existing research results do not support either the claim that speaker body build (height and weight) is related to pitch level or the claim that listeners are capable of precisely estimating the height and weight of speakers on the basis of vocal characteristics (Graddol and Swann, 1983: 354).

Cultural differences between men's and women's voice pitch

Some research results show that speaking voice pitch can be influenced by cultural expectations rather than physical factors. In a 1972 comparison between Polish and American males, Majewski *et al.* found that Polish males' average speaking voice pitch is noticeably higher than that of American males. Difference in physical size between Polish and American men did not prove to be significantly related to mean speaking voice pitch. The researchers concluded that cultural differences may be a contributing factor. Support for cultural influence can also be found in Loveday's (1981) investigation of Japanese and (British) English male and female speakers. The evidence was strong despite the small number of subjects in the study. The Japanese males voice pitch levels were much lower than those of the British males. In contrast, voice pitch levels of Japanese females were conspicuously higher than that of British females. Although Loveday did not measure his informants' physical size, it can be expected that there is a significant difference in physical size between the Japanese and British groups. However, the Japanese males' extremely low voice pitch levels do not appear to be related to their smaller body size. Only Japanese females' remarkably high pitch levels may be explained in terms of their physical size. Overall, Loveday makes a convincing case that cultural differences in social expectation of gender play an important role in voice pitch differences.

It has been claimed that speakers choose speaking voice pitch ranges that suit their social identity as well as physical attributes associated with sex and body size. Differences in men's and women's speaking voice pitch appear to be caused by an interaction between physical and cultural determinants. In a 1983 study, Graddol and Swann explored these questions further. They were concerned that a correlation between physical difference and speaking voice pitch may not show up in single-sex samples. Graddoll and Swann re-investigated the relationship between height, weight and speaking voice pitch by utilizing longer samples of speech consisting of passage and constructed dialogue produced by socially homogeneous speakers. Contrary to the results of other studies of body size, their research results suggest that speaker height is related to average speaking voice pitch in male but not female speakers. Graddol and Swann theorize that this discrepancy may reflect the fact that cultural influences may be stronger for women's voice pitch than for that of men's when reading a passage. In both male and female subjects' 'dialogue' reading, however, correlations between median speaking voice pitch and speaker height/weight were not significant. Graddol and Swann concluded that more variable intonation patterns utilized in reading the constructed dialogue exert a major influence over the statistical distribution of speaking fundamental frequency. This implies that the relationship between physical size and their voice pitch during naturally occurring conversations may virtually be irrelevant. Therefore, in my treatise, I disregard the potential link between physical size and voice pitch among same sex speakers and explore the relationship obtaining between voice pitch and non-physical factors such as culture.

It is often thought that Japan and America exemplify completely opposite sets of cultural norms and consequently offer excellent sample pools by which to compare and contrast abiding social variables. For example, these societies represent cultures with contrasting values such as individualism and collectivism. Individualism is 'stands for a society in which the ties between individuals are loose: everyone is expected to look after himself or herself and his or her immediate family only' (Hofstede, 1994: 261). By contrast, collectivism 'stands for a society in which people from birth onwards are integrated into strong cohesive ingroups, which throughout people's lifetime continue to protect them in exchange for unquestioning loyalty' (Hofstede, 1994: 260). The present volume, however, does not explicitly incorporate the dichotomy of individualism and collectivism into the explanations for cultural differences in voice pitch modulation. The dimension of individualism and collectivism, which Hofstede (1980; 1983) popularized based on the results of his large scale cross-cultural comparative study, has become a default concept that explains a wide variety of cultural differences in human behavior (Kagitcibasi, 1994). Nevertheless, I found it crucial to consider such concepts as emotion, politeness, the *uchi* (inner)/*soto* (outer) dichotomy, *amae* (Doi, 1981) and *wakimae* (Ide, 1989) in comparing the cultural differences in behaviors between the people of these societies. In addition, it must be noted that the cultures which I refer to in this volume are the mainstream American (Anglo-American based) and Japanese cultures. The issue of cultural and linguistic diversities within American and Japanese societies is outside of the scope of my investigation.

Impressionistic observations of voice pitch

Observations of men's and women's voice pitch have been commonly impressionistic by the general public, contributing to perceptual stereo-types of this prosodic feature. These impressionistic commentaries, however, do tell us about our attitudes toward certain voice pitch characteristics. There are ample impressionistic depictions of both sexes' voice characteristics recorded in various types of literature across American and Japanese cultures prior to and after the onset of acoustic phonetic research on voice pitch. The general perception of men's and women's voice pitches across cultures is fairly similar: men's voice pitch is low while women's is high with emphatic intonational variations. However, there appears to be a slight variance between the subject societies as to how individuals feel about high-pitched voice. This attitudinal difference, in turn, was found to surface in the acoustically measured voice pitch modulation patterns obtained from Japanese and American speakers. Chapter 1 contains a collection of these impressionistic portrayals of men's and women's voice pitch characteristics as found in novels, handbooks, and scholars' comments from as early as eleventh century Japan as well as seventeenth century America.

Acoustic analyses of voice pitch

Acoustic phonetic investigations of voice pitch were initiated in the early twentieth century in both America and Japan. A number of these researches contributed to both confirming and reconsidering the impressionistic remarks on men's and women's voice pitches made earlier. These early researches mainly utilized sustained vowels, passages, and constructed dialogues. Chapter 2 includes an extensive review of these investigations which focused on relatively young groups of speakers (ages ranging between 17 and 39) conducted in both nations of Japan and America thus far. One of two major universal behavioral concepts which this book invokes in interpreting voice pitch modulation variations is that of emotion. Chapter 2 ends with a section that introduces numerous research studies previously conducted on the correlation between voice cues and emotion types.

Chapter 3 begins with an introduction of comparative examinations of Japanese and American voice pitch performed by previous researchers. They also obtained their results from passages and constructed dialogues read by informants. For a full understanding of the functions of paralinguistic features (such as pitch), however, systematic examinations of actual usage in communication contexts are necessary. It was not until the end of the twentieth century that a few isolated voice pitch researchers finally began examining spontaneously produced conversational speech data obtained from conversational speech. This treatise focuses on my research which examined data obtained from conversational speech in the late 1990s and early 2000s using an original procedure. Moreover, earlier research results mainly presented informants' average voice pitch in terms of Hertz or semitones. I analyzed the complexity of voice pitch fluctuations by breaking down conversational sentences into intonation groups and painstakingly parsing more detailed pitch modulation patterns in terms of this intonation unit. In do doing, I was able to see the variability of voice pitch modulation that is based on social relationship held between the speakers and interlocutors. In addition, voice pitch must be systematically examined in terms of how it is perceived rather than how it is instrumentally measured. The effort was made to present voice pitch as it is expressed in values on the ERB-scale,[2] considered the most appropriate calculus for understanding human speech perception.

Voice pitch and emotion

Historically, the topic of emotion and its expression has been a major concern for researchers in the fields of both psychology and linguistics. Scholars in these fields have long been aware that human feelings are expressed vocally and kinetically. These academicians have postulated the manner in which those emotions are expressed. As early as the 1920s, they also began conducting numerous experiments which generated fairly regular correlates between vocal or facial expressions and types of emotions. It would seem that most of these researchers have little doubt by now that certain vocal and kinetic gestures are closely linked to both physical and psychological states of consciousness. The expression of emotion is one of the key concepts which this volume explores in an attempt to explain the variations of voice pitch modulation found across culture and gender in my study. Among the vocal cues investigated by researchers, voice pitch has been regarded as a major cue determining both the degree and types of emotion expressed. In Chapter 4, I will briefly adduce research on the nature of the expression of emotion (conducted in the field of psychology) as well as linguistic approaches to the patterns of intonation (pitch modulation) in expressing emotion. I will also indulge in a discussion of theories developed for comprehending the concept of emotion and cross-cultural studies on facial expressions of emotion formally conducted by D. Matsumoto and his collaborators (Matsumoto 1991, 1996; Matsumoto, Kudoh, Scherer, and Wallbot 1988). Doi's discussion of Japanese psychology involving the notions of self-indulgence (*amae*) and restraint (*enryo*) will be also highlighted in this chapter. *Amae* is arguably 'self-indulgence'; its ultimate expression is an infant's behavior with its mother. *Enryo*, on the other hand, means 'distant consideration' or 'restraint'. In the parent–child relationship there is no *enryo* – the relationship is permeated with *amae*. In other relationships, the degree of *enryo* decreases proportionately with intimacy and increases with distance. This pair of psychological concepts plays a critical role in elucidating the voice pitch movement variations which the Japanese informants demonstrated in my investigation. I conclude Chapter 4 by explaining how I interpret the degree of speakers' expressions of emotion with regard to voice pitch movement width, drawing on the comparative investigation, which I report in Chapter 3.

Voice pitch and politeness

Politeness is a concept that is 'basic to the production of social order and a precondition of human cooperation' (Gumperz, 1987: xiii). During the last three decades, matters pertaining to the concept of politeness generated great interest in the fields of sociolinguistics, pragmatics, applied linguistics, social psychology, conversation analysis and anthropology. Scholars in differing fields have variously understood politeness phenomena. Although the understanding of the notion of politeness may differ from one scholar to another, from language to language and between cultures, what is shared by all is a strong belief in its universal presence and significance (Brown and Levinson, 1987: 1). I find it essential to also adopt the concept of politeness in construing the variations of voice pitch modulation found across culture and gender. The section fleetingly explains that the earliest treatment of the concept of politeness as described by Lakoff in 1973 and the most thoroughly investigated model by Brown and Levinson basically suggest two types of politeness. These are formal/negative and camaraderie/positive politeness. Ide fundamentally confirms that the system of Japanese honorifics belongs to the former type of politeness (formal/negative politeness) without the strategic intentions that Brown and Levison argue the notion of politeness entails. She introduces the concept of '*wakimae*' (discernment) to account for the usage of such formal linguistic forms in Japanese.

In Japan, the politeness mode which the Japanese people utilize is a formal/deferential or negative politeness style when conversing with unfamiliar interlocutors. In this type of politeness, they employ honorifics linguistically to keep both distance from and show deference toward the interlocutors. The chapter once again herein considers Doi's discussion of Japanese psychological notions of *enryo* ('restraint') and *amae* ('self-indulgence'). When *enryo* is necessary and *amae* is absent, the exaggeration of one's emotions and feelings appears to be not so freely allowed in Japanese culture. By contrast, when the same Japanese individuals converse with familiar interlocutors, they drop honorifics and simply use plain forms (camaraderie/positive politeness style of speech). In this type of interaction, *enryo* is much less necessary and *amae* in fact increases. The expression of emotion becomes easier in this type of social relationship.

In my investigation, the pitch movement employed in the former type of conversation with unfamiliar interlocutors (where a formal/deferential or negative politeness style was employed) was relatively narrow. My argument is that this occurred as a result of the speakers' hesitancy to express feelings fully in a less familiar social relationship which inhered between them. I derived this view from previous emotion studies (mentioned in Chapter 1) indicating that a narrow pitch movement connotes the absence of emotional involvement, a condition which researchers characterized as 'bored' and 'uninterested'. Such a suppression of emotional engagement, I believe, can be either strategic example of formal/negative mode of politeness or conventionalized form of politeness as in the case of usage of honorifics which Ide affirms. In contradistinction, in the conversation with familiar interlocutors, Japanese informants' voice pitch movements widened. The absence of honorifics indicated that they are functioning in a camaraderie/positive politeness mode. I surmised that their use of widened pitch movements was a manifestation of the informants' inclination to share their feelings more fully with the interlocutors. This self-same usage of widened pitch movements concomitantly appears to reflect on their tendency to express their 'selves' (since an expression of emotions is societally acceptable and expected n this latter situation). Earlier studies also confirm an association between a wide pitch movement and feelings labeled as 'elation' (Chapter 2). The display of these latter emotions, I attest, is a much less strategic and more spontaneous form of camaraderie/positive politeness since it is caused by an increase in *amae* ('self-indulgence'). It also appears to me that releasing such emotions is somewhat distant from complying with convention such as utilizing socially expected linguistic forms of the Japanese language as Ide avers. Two discourse analyses, which use conversational excerpts by Japanese informants in my studies, demonstrating the point of my argument will be presented here.

Chapter 5, at this point, ventures into a consideration of issues of politeness with respect to gender. It first examines theories and claims about women's politeness in four diverse societies (America, New Zealand, Central American Indian Village (Tenejapa), and Japan). In America, New Zealand and Tzeltal (the dialect spoken in the Tenejapa), women reportedly use both types of formal/negative and camaraderie/positive politeness. However, the latter type of politeness more extensively by females than males. Even in Japan (a nation often referred to as a prototypical culture with a strong emphasis on formal/negative politeness in interpersonal communication) the use of camaraderie/positive politeness devices by women has also been reported. This is particularly true of those who wear the mantle of authority in the workplace. The work of Lakoff, Holmes, Brown and Takano will be reviewed here. The chapter also includes Brown's and Levinson's discussion of what they found are prosodic characteristics of men's and women's speech with regard to camaraderie/positive politeness. In so doing, I argue that women's tendency to choose camaraderie/positive politeness style of communication is one plausible explanation for the difference in maximal voice pitch modulation demonstrated between American male and female speakers. I will provide herein additional discourse analyses, derived from conversational excerpts of both American and Japanese female informants in my studies, underscoring the thrust of my argument.

Voice pitch, politeness and gender

In Japan, in the 1990s it was reported by researchers such as Okamoto and Y. Matsumoto that women (both young and middle-aged) had begun using a less feminine linguistic styles. As far as voice pitch modulation is concerned, however, we may continue to see Japanese women utilizing a high-pitched voice due to persistent societal expectation to project a feminine image. These women may be desirous of being perceived as feminine and thus attractive. It may be that the esthetic value placed by general societal preference on women's high-pitched voice (as pointed out in the 1956 novel by Kawabata and 1969 comments by Mashimo) is subliminally perpetuated in Japanese women's minds. Impressionistic accounts of voice pitch in Japanese which I located never seemingly attached any stigma upon high-pitched voice by women in this society. This section of Chapter 5 also briefly reviews Van Bezooijen's 1995 study as well as the 2000 Sugihara and Katsurada's surveys which concomitantly support my reasoning for the phenomenon of Japanese women's usage of a high-pitched voice. Chapter 5 also outlines here the 1995 New York Times article the subject of which was Japanese elevator girls' unnaturally voice pitch. I also allude to Kasuya's 1995 investigation (reported in *The Daily Yomiuri*) of Japanese female newscasters' voice pitch in the same literary breath. These articles are remarked upon in this context in order to present Japanese women's apparent ambivalent feelings with respect to their speaking voice pitch.

By contrast, the American women seems to be lowering their overall lower voice pitch level. This section of Chapter 5 proceeds to summarize the view that American women's voice pitch has lowered in the last century. It is speculated that a historical stigma attached to the high-pitched voice in American society played a role in lowering American women's voice pitch. This stigma is implied in impressionistic accounts of American men's and women's voice characteristics (Chapter 1).

With regard to median voice pitch movement widths, I discovered that they do not show conspicuous differences across gender when expressed in what is considered the most appropriate frequency scale (the ERB) for human speech perception. Female speakers, nevertheless, do sporadically utilize extremely wide pitch movements or movements occurring at the higher end of women's register. Women appear to exhibit these pitch characteristics most conspicuously in conversational settings. It is my premise that people in both cultures are conditioned to pay attention to those few extreme pitch movements in depicting women' speech style. The former types of pitch movement is characterized as 'swoopy', the latter as 'squeaky'. This section of Chapter 5 briefly explores this issue.

In public, Japanese males may continue to be interested in projecting a traditionally masculine image. Their voice pitch movements are relatively narrow and average lowest voice pitch level continues to be low (even slightly lower than the corresponding American males). These are consistent with Seward's 1968 observation of Japanese men's efforts to emphasize the masculinity of their speech through usage of a deep-voice. However, their voice pitch movements became widened considerably when they interacted with familiar interlocutors. Furthermore, their maximal pitch movements were nearly twice as wide as those of American males. This section of Chapter 5 recounts how I interpreted these findings in terms of camaraderie/positive politeness normally expected in a situation in Japan where *amae* and comfort of expressing oneself are extant.

American men in general may be under pressure not to speak with a high-pitched voice. They may use voice pitch movements much narrower than those of their Japanese counterparts in order to accomplish this. The last part of Chapter 5 links these findings to a tendency to avoid camaraderie/positive politeness as well as a potential inexpressiveness associated with the classic image of American masculinity. Moreover, a discourse analysis of one of the conversations by American males combined with voice pitch measurements revealed that one pair appeared to be interested in engaging in camaraderie/positive style of politeness with emphatic expressiveness. This last section of Chapter 5 presents a brief overview of my interpretations of male speakers (across cultures): these speakers seemingly possess the ability to expand their voice pitch ranges *if and when* the situation (as well as the nature of the relationship between speech participants) call for a more expressive camaraderie style of interaction.

Notes

1. Beclard. Larynx. *Dict. ency, des Sci. Med.* 554–65. Ellis did not provide the year which this encyclopedia was published.
2. The scale which uses both linear and logarithmic scales. The details concerning this scale are described in Chapter 3.

I   Impressionistic Observations of Voice and Voice Pitch

This chapter contains my collection of the impressionistic portrayals of men's and women's voice pitch characteristics in Japan and the United States as found in novels, handbooks, and scholars' comments. The Japanese materials date back from as early as eleventh-century Japan while American materials date back only to the seventeenth century. Observations of men's and women's voice pitch by the general public contributed to our perceptual stereotypes of this prosodic feature as they were based on their impressionistic consciousness. These impressionistic commentaries, however, do tell us about both similarities and differences in our attitudes toward certain voice pitch characteristics of the two cultures of Japan and America. There are ample impressionistic depictions of both sexes' voice characteristics recorded in various types of literature across these cultures prior to and after the onset of acoustic phonetic research on voice pitch. At a glance, the general perception of men's and women's voice pitches across cultures may appear fairly similar. That is, men's voice pitch is low whereas women's is high with emphatic intonational variations. However, how individuals in each culture feel about high-pitched voice seem to differ between the subject societies. I found this attitudinal difference to surface in the acoustically measured voice pitch modulation patterns, which I obtained from my Japanese and American informants. More details on my finding will be given in the following chapters.

Novels

Japan

Numerous examples of depictions of Japanese men's and women's voice characteristics are found in Japanese literature. I chose the eleventh-century novel, *The Tale of Genji*, and the nineteenth-century novels such as *Tales of the Supernatural, Drifting Clouds, Pagoda, Botchan, The Bearded Samurai* and *Snow Country*. All of these novels and tales have continued to be regarded as both popular and canonical in Japan and thus are. They are likely to reflect people's cultural attitudes.

In 1969 Mashimo (1969: 8), a Japanese linguist, noted that differences in male and female speech styles gradually emerged over a long period of time – conspicuous contrasts were not recognized by commentators until the fourteenth century in Japan. According to him, in the Heian Period (794–1192 AD) it was considered good manners if Japanese women of higher station did not talk in loud voices during conversation (Mashimo, 1969: 39). Those women who could talk so faintly that their voices were almost inaudible seemed thereby to attract men. Thus, this manner of speaking quietly was regarded as an important element which contributed to making women appear beautiful and docile (Mashimo, 1969: 39). Mashimo's observations were based on the following extract from *The Tale of Genji* (written in the early eleventh century), which depicts this aspect of women's speech style of that era:

> In their letters they (young and pretty women) choose the most harmless topics, but yet contrive to colour the very texture of the written signs with a tenderness that vaguely disquiets us. But such a one, when we have at last secured a meeting, will speak so low that she can scarcely be heard, and the few sentences that she murmurs beneath serve only to make her more mysterious than before. (Murasaki, 1960: 25)

Note that the characterization of voice as 'low' here meant 'low in volume' not necessarily 'low in pitch.' A Chinese character which literal meaning is 'high' contained in the words in Japanese that express voice characteristics is mainly understood as 'loud' or 'high in volume.'

I found one scene in *Ugetsu Monogatari (Tales of the Supernatural)* by Akinari Ueda, written in 1776, where the expression literally meaning 'voice being high' was used to describe 'loud voice.' In one of the tales entitled 'Bewitched,' a father hears his two sons quarrelling. Their voice was portrayed as 'loud' despite that the actual word used to depict this voice contains a Chinese character meaning 'high.'

> Their father heard the loud quarrelsome voice. (Ueda, 1974: 28)

In *Ukigumo (Drifting Clouds)* (1887–9), Japan's first modern novel authored by Futabatei, Shimei, an expression, which contains the Chinese character meaning 'high' but is interpreted as 'loud,' occurs repeatedly. Bunzo Utsumi, the male protagonist, was practically engaged with his cousin, Osei. However, as a result of the loss of his job in the lowest ranks of the government bureaucracy, his marriage has become impossible. Osei is now affectionate toward Noboru Honda, Bunzo's former colleague who is more promising than Bunzo (Ryan 1990: Introduction).

There are several scenes where Osei and Noboru laugh at Bunzo in the novel. They do this with loud laughter. The expression used to describe their laughter literally means 'high laughter' in the Japanese language. In the novel, nevertheless, it does not mean that they laughed in a high-pitched voice. Rather, the volume of the laughter was high, and thus loud.

> With a slight bow Bunzo sprang to his feet and left the room. He
> had only gone a few steps when <u>a loud chorus of laughter</u> (by
> Osei and Bunzo) burst out behind him. (Ryan, 1990: 286)

Moreover, the compound word with the literal meaning of 'low voice' in Japanese is interpreted as 'soft voice.' In the scene where Osei recites Chinese poems, she is portrayed as doing this in a soft voice rather than a low voice.

> They heard her (Osei's) joking with Onabe in the hall and then
> softly reciting Chinese poems in her room. (Ryan, 1990: 305)

However, in another scene, one novel character's voice pitch level as well as loudness is actually depicted. Omasa, Osei's mother, while speaking with Bunzo about her daughter, changes the tone of her voice quickly at one point.

> 'I'm certain that it was.' She <u>cried</u>, cutting him off abruptly. Her
> voice resumed its <u>normal tone</u> as she went on. (Ryan, 1990: 331)

Although the verb depicting Omasa's action in the first sentence was translated as 'cried,' the expression in Japanese used here precisely means 'said in a higher tone than usual.' The verb used to describe her voice in the following sentence means 'to fall,' which portrays Omasa's voice pitch actually lowering to the normal level.

There are two more similar examples found in Rohan Koda's *Goju no to* (Pagoda) written in 1891. In the following scenes, 'loud laugh' by two Carpenters, Genta and Seikichi, is expressed in Japanese using the Chinese character meaning 'high.'

> Seikichi forgot his manners and grew too comfortable with Genta's
> affable mood and Okichi's hospitality. He emptied the sake cup as
> often as it was filled until his ruddy face took on the color of ripe
> cherry. He <u>laughed loudly</u>, put on pompous airs, gossiped about
> his colleagues, ... (Koda, 1982: 60)

> Genta, too discreet to reveal his true feelings, offered a sake cup
> to Seikichi and <u>laughed loudly</u>, 'What are you mumbling about,
> Seikichi?' (Koda, 1982: 62)

The examples I have given show that this Chinese character (whose literal meaning is 'high') is mostly understood in Japanese as 'loud' or 'high in volume'. Thus, the characterization of voice as 'low' means 'low in volume' or 'soft voice' as opposed to being 'low in pitch'.

I now provide an instance of a classic example of literally 'high-pitched' voice found in one of these novels. The narrator remarks that this voice, as used by a female character, is a 'beautiful' one. There is an intriguing portrayal of a high-pitched Japanese women in the novel, *Snow Country*, written by Yasunari Kawabata, Japan's first novelist who won the Nobel Prize for Literature in 1968. *Snow Country* is known to have attained the award owing partly to its expressions for the essence of the Japanese mind. There is a scene where the male protagonist, Shimamura (a critic of Western dances living in Tokyo) first sees Yoko, one of the geisha girls whom he will get to know better later in the snowy hot spring resort place.

> 'Is my brother here now?' Yoko looked our over the snow-covered
> platform. 'See that he behaves himself'. <u>It was such a beautiful
> voice</u> that it struck one as sad. <u>In all its high resonance</u> it seems to
> come echoing back across the snowy night. (Kawabata, 1956: 5)

In the novel, Yoko is depicted as a woman whose serene voice has a fragile, unreal kind of beauty. Kawabata, who portrayed the quintessential beauty of Japan in this masterpiece, characterized the 'high-pitched voice' articulated by of his female character as 'beautiful'.

Moreover, I found depictions of various types of stereotypically masculine voices used by Japanese warrior characters in *The Bearded Samurai*, written by Rohan Koda. The novel is a historical tale that takes place in the mid-sixteenth century, the Warring States period, which was a time of social upheaval, political adventure, and frequent military conflict in Japan. The setting is the battle of Nagashino fought in 1575 between the Takeda army and the combined Oda-Tokugawa forces (Koda, 1982: 17). In the tale, the most central warrior characters speak in various types of stereotypically masculine voices such as a 'deep' voice, a 'somber' tone, a 'rugged' voice, and a 'forceful' voice. They also 'growled,' 'bawled' and 'barked' in numerous scenes. In the scene where Lord Katsuyori shamefully displays his temper, General Yamagata is shocked into silence.

> Yamagata hung his head for a long time. At last, <u>his deep voice</u>
> suppressed, his impassioned face blanched by grief, and .... (Koda,
> 1982: 171)

Another depiction occurs in the 1906 novel *Botchan* by Soseki
Natsume (1968) when the main protagonist Botchan first meets the
Assistant Principle of the high school where he has been appointed to
teach. Botchan notices that the Assistant Principal, although a man,
speaks in a gentle voice like that of women.

> He had a sweet caressing voice a lady would be proud of being
> possessor. (34)

Botchan gives the Assistant Principle the nickname 'Red-shirt' simply
because he is known to wear only a red flannel shirt all year around.
Botchan further comments on the Assistant Principle's voice as follows:

> Red-shirt is the possessor of such <u>a sweet tongue</u> as to give the
> hearer uneasiness. No one can tell him from a female by the mere
> ring of his voice. If a man, he should have <u>a manly voice</u>. Is not he
> graduate of the Imperial University? I, a mere graduate of the
> Physics School, have a much <u>bolder voice</u>. It is a shame for a
> *bungakushi* (Bachelor of Arts) to have such <u>an effeminate voice</u>!
> (Natsume, 1968: 66–7)

> I have an aversion to Red-shirt because of his voice. I can assure
> you that <u>his natural voice is rough</u>, but from affectation he is trying
> hard to show people <u>how sweet his voice</u> is. (Natsume, 1968: 80)

Note that none of the negative descriptions used by Botchan to depict Red-shirt's effeminate voice refers specifically to a 'high-pitched.'
However, Botcham does specifically comment that an educated man in
a high-ranking position should not speak in a soft, sweet, effeminate
voice. Further, the protagonist mentions that a woman who possesses
such a sweet caressing voice should be proud of that voice.

The characterization of voice as 'low' means mostly 'low in volume'
or 'soft voice' not necessarily 'low in pitch' in Japanese. This appears to
be consistent regardless of the gender of the novels' characters. Female
voices are often portrayed as 'soft voices.' When the female character's
voice is described literally as 'high-pitched,' it is regarded as 'beautiful.'
By contrast, we see in these novels that stereotypically masculine voices
are expected for men who are in commanding positions. Therefore,
effeminate voices utilized by such men are not tolerated without necessarily mentioning that feminine voices are high-pitched.

The United States

I found depictions of men's and women's voice characteristics in a number of classic American literary works of the nineteenth, including *Little Women, The Portrait of a Lady*, and *The Adventures of Tom Sawyer*. In these novels, female protagonists' voices are depicted as relatively 'low' not 'high.' The authors of these novels (regardless of their gender of the author) take a negative view of a high-pitched voice in their female characters. By contrast, male characters of these novels generally speak with 'low voice,' and sometimes 'loud.' In *The Portrait of a Lady*, the protagonist's husband possesses 'a perfect pitched-voice.'

In this section of the chapter I show that in the aforementioned novels, the major female protagonists' voices are depicted as relatively 'low' (as opposed to 'high'). By contrast, other secondary female characters with high-pitched voices are generally portrayed negatively. I also allude to the fact that in one of the novels, a male protagonist's 'low voice' is considered by the author as a 'standard voice.'

Little Women, the popular 1868 American novel by Louisa May Alcott, is known to have been based on the author's own experiences growing up as a young women with three other sisters. The novel depicts the voice changes of the March sisters as they grow older. Meg, the oldest daughter is described as having a sweet voice 'like a flute' when she is 16 or 17 years old. By the time she is 22, she has a 'tender voice; voice full of motherly love, gratitude, and humility.' Amy, the youngest girl, 'chirped like a cricket' when she was 12 years old. However, by the time she turned 17 or so, she speaks with 'a calm, cool voice; it was in a voice that could be beautifully soft and kind when she chose to make it so.' Her voice has 'a new tenderness.' Jo, Josephine the protagonist, already is speaking 'in a low voice' when she is 15. Nevertheless, her voice becomes even 'lower' by the time she is 18 years old.

The only older female character whose voice is depicted in the novel is Aunt March. She speaks with a shrill voice. Mr March, the sisters' father, is described as having a 'fatherly' voice. Mr Laurence, the Marches' loving and kind next-door neighbor possesses a gruff voice. His grandson, Laurie speaks in a low, kind voice. Laurie's tutor, Mr Brooke is a man with a pleasant voice. Mr Bhaer, a professor from Germany to whom Jo marries, talks with a strong voice. In addition, one of Laurie's most elegant male college friends has a masculine voice.

Mark Twain's *Adventures of Tom Sawyer* was published in 1876 and quickly became regarded as one of the classic works of American literature. Three major male characters are portrayed as speaking in a low voice at least once in the story: Huckleberry Finn, the son of the town drunk, Dr Robinson, a respected local physician; and Injun Joe, a villainous man who commits murder. The following are relevant passages:

> The doctor [Dr Robinson] put the lantern at the head of the grave,
> and came and sat down with his back against one of the elm trees.
> He was so close the boys could have touched him. 'Hurry, men!'
> he said <u>in a low voice</u>. 'The moon might come out at any mo-
> ment.' (Twain, 1998: 76)

> Now there was a voice, a very low voice of Injun Joe's:
> 'Damn her! maybe she's got company, there's lights, late as it is.'
> 'I can't see any.' (Twain, 1998: 201)

> Huck's <u>scared voice answered in a low tone</u>:
> 'Please let me in! It's only Huck Finn!' (Twain, 1998: 204)

However, there are no description of female characters' voices found in the novel except for that of the voice of Aunt Polly, Tom's aunt and guardian.

> Aunt Polly knelt down and prayed for Tom so touchingly, so
> appealingly, and with such measureless love in her words and her
> <u>old trembling voice</u>, that he was weltering in tears again long
> before she was through. (Twain, 1998: 117)

The Portrait of a Lady, Henry James' late nineteenth-century classic, contains intriguing depictions of men and women's voice characteristics. James' novels are esteemed for their sensitively drawn portraits of women. The novel does not portray the voice of the heroin, Isabel, as high. Her voice is depicted twice in the novel as relatively lower. However, Isabel's close friend Henrietta Stackpole, a feminist journalist who does not believe that women need men in order to be happy, has her voice portrayed quite differently. First of all, her voice is depicted as clear, high, and loud.

> Ralph saw at a glance that she [Henrietta] was as crisp and new
> and comprehensive as a first issue before the folding. From top to
> toe she had probably no misprint. She spoke in <u>a clear, high voice-
> a voice not rich but loud</u>; (James, 188: 162)

Henrietta's voice quality is depicted as leaving a strong impression on other people. One example is the scene where Isabel's husband (Gilbert Osmond), who dislikes Henrietta, complains:

> I don't see her [Henrietta], but I hear her; I hear her all day long.
> Her voice is in my ears; I can't get rid of it. I know exactly what

> she says, and every inflexion of the tone in which she says it.
> (James, 188: 364)

James describes another female character, Countess Gemini (Gilbert Osmond's sister), as having a high, strained voice.

> There was a certain relief presently, in hearing the high, strained voice of her sister-in-law. The Countess too, apparently, had been thinking the thing out, but had arrived at a different conclusion from Isabel. (James, 188: 395)

In the same novel, male characters' voices are described as 'loud,' 'harsh,' 'kind,' 'mild,' and 'low.' For example, Isabel's brother-in-law (a New York lawyer) possesses a loud voice. Isabel's husband, however, speaks in a mild, kind, low, and deep voice. Strikingly, her husband's voice is also depicted as 'perfectly-pitched voice'. The implication is that the male voice is regarded as the standard or neutral voice pitch.

> Indeed he [Goodwood] scarcely knew what Osmond was talking about; he wanted to be alone with Isabel, and that idea spoke louder to him than her husband's perfectly-pitched voice. (James, 188: 374)

In the canonical American literature which I examined, the words selected to depict female characters' voices are combined with expressions containing undesirable connotations. This includes 'shrill,' 'high and loud,' and 'high, strained.' These terms appear to convey 'loudness and tension' associated with high pitch. By contrast, male characters' voices are consistently described as 'low voice,' but are never portrayed as-objectionable voice.

Etiquette Books/Handbooks

Japan

Etiquette books and handbooks which presumably are meant to teach proper behaviors to members of a society are excellent sources touching upon what men's and women's voice (pitch) characteristics optimally should be. This advice, in turn, can tell us about how men and women may have actually spoken. I initially introduce excerpts from resources dating back to the thirteenth century in Japan: *Booklet for Nursemaid, Women's Moderation*, and *Hagakure*. In these books, women and warriors are instructed not to speak loudly (the implication being that they have a natural tendency to speak in a loud tone).

A thirteenth century precept embodied in *Menoto no Soshi* (*Booklet for Nursemaids*) is that daughters of the noble class should not speak in loud voices. Nursemaids are specifically instructed to rear daughters of the privileged class in such a manner that they will learn to speak only in a low-volumed (and thus quiet) voice (*Menoto no Soshi*, 1911: 35) as seen below:

> As for raising daughters, when they become around ten years old, you may want to present them to the public. You are advised to raise them so that they would be a bit cheerful with *low-volumed* [and thus quiet: my emphasis] voice. Do not allow them to romp about as they desire, speak carelessly, … in general, keep in mind that they would not talk loudly in high-volumed voices. (My translation)

Mashimo (1969: 40), a linguist who initially examined Japanese women's language and its education in 1949, suggests that an important part of the formal training of higher-class women was focused on proper voice modulation. Therefore, in seventeenth-century Japan, precepts exclusively intended to teach women how to behave (such as *Onna Choho Ki* [*Records of Women's Important Treasures*] by Johaku Namura), began appearing one after another. Mashimo's list of more than 30 instructional manuals of this type published between 1692 and 1868 included sections pertaining to how women should speak (Mashimo, 1969: 112–48). For example, *Onna Chuyo* (*Women's Moderation*), the eighteenth century text written by Gyokushi Uemura (1910: 147) states that:

> as for the second comportment of women, the language, watch your tongue. You would be considered incompetent [unskillful] if you use vulgar language. Choice of words [use of words] should be neither strong nor playful, and the voice should not be loud/high-volumed. (My translation)

In pre-modern Japanese society, the use of women's loud voices was clearly stigmatized. It is speculated that the reason for the disapproval of such vocal characteristics is connected with differences in women's images based on social class of that period. Such disfavored vocal qualities were possibly associated with the speech style used by laywomen who lived in the inner cities (Mashimo, 1969: 41). These women's speech styles may have been tolerated because of their neglected (or relatively carefree) upbringings in an urban environment. By contrast, women from well-to-do families were compelled to use only soft voices at low amplitude levels. It can be conjectured that the latter vocal traits were identified with more educated and thus emotionally controlled images of women in the privileged classes.

It is noteworthy that the main concern in molding Japanese women's speech in these handbooks dealt with the loudness of voice, rather than its pitch levels or intonational fluctuations. Under the Buddhist and Confucian influence Japanese women were for centuries encouraged to behave in such a way that they appeared gentle and quiet (not impulsive or emotional). This may have contributed to Japanese female voice characteristics and possibly also led to suppressed expression of emotion. Japanese women, especially those of a higher class, may have learned they would be censured if they did not exercise such practices.

For men's speech training, I looked for teachings in *Nan Choho Ki* (*Records of Men's Valuable Treasures*) by Juhaku Namura (who is also the author of *Onna Choho Ki* [*Records of Women's Important Treasures*]). The book contains numerous mentions of how certain linguistic expressions differ regionally. However, I did not find any remark on how men in medieval Japanese society were expected to use their voice.

I also searched for allusions on men's speech in *Hagakure* (*The Book of The Samurai*). The book contains the following instruction:

> <u>Training to speak properly can be done by correcting one's speech when at home</u>. (Yamamoto, 1979: 41)

Unfortunately, the *Hagakure* provides little specific instruction with regard to how Samurai should speak. There is one passage, however, in which a priest is quoted concerning how Samurai should <u>not</u> speak:

> Meeting with people should be a matter of quickly grasping their temperament and reacting appropriately to this person and that. Especially with an extremely argumentative person, after yielding considerably one should argue him down with superior logic, but without <u>sounding harsh</u>, and in a fashion that will allow no resentment to be left afterwards. This is a function of both the heart and words. This was an opinion given by a priest concerning personal encounters. (Yamamoto, 1979: 65)

Indeed, Samurai were discouraged from speaking. The following statement depicts the virtue of reticence.

> The essentials of speaking are in not speaking at all. If you think that you can finish something without speaking, finish it without saying a single word. If there is something that cannot be accomplished without speaking, one should speak with few words, in a

> way that will accord well with reason. To open one's mouth
> indiscriminately brings shame, and there are many times when
> people will turn their backs on such a person. (Yamamoto, 1979:
> 162)

Additionally, I searched for further teachings with regard to Samurai Warriors speech in Nitobe's Bushido: *The Soul of Japan* (1905). In describing the characters and teachings of *Bushido*, Nitobe indicates that in order to display a strong disposition one must show 'no sign of joy or anger.' This was a phrase often used in instructing samurai to suppress their emotion. Even the most natural affections, such as expressions of love for family members, need to be controlled. Samurai are told that calmness of behavior and serenity of mind should not be sullied by any kind of passion (Nitobe, 1905: 94). However, Nitobe does not refer, in any part of his book, to how samurai *should* speak.

There are two intriguing articles written in 1995 and 1996 by major newspapers on the subject of what constitutes appropriate levels of voice pitch for Japanese female department store employees and newscasters.

The 1995 *New York Times* article by Kristof reports that the so-called 'elevator girls' who work in department stores in Japan are *trained* to speak in an unnaturally high-pitched voice. The article describes how Hiromi Saito and 18 other female elevator operators use a falsetto voice pitch to announce the floors at the Mitsukoshi Department Store in Tokyo's Ginza district. Miss Saito, as chief of the unit, trains the new employees to raise their pitch. According to her, girls with lower pitched voices struggle initially. However, within a month they learn to transform their voice and within three months they acquire completely different voices.

This *New York Times* article also includes an opinion of a computer company employee (Harumi Yamamoto) in Tokyo who believes that her voice naturally rises when she wants to be polite. She maintains that her voices in the office and at home are totally different. High pitch is definitely associated with the Japanese preoccupation with courtesy in Japan. Japanese women sound normal to an American ear in ordinary conversation at home or with friends. However, according to the article, the same women may apologize to their boss or customer on the phone using a voice off their register.

The *New York Times* article also describes the importance of voice pitch for female broadcasters. It describes the case of Miyuki Morita, whose voice was too 'somber.' She was rejected when she first tried to enter broadcasting as a disk jockey. When she eventually found a job with a television station in northern Japan, she had to try imitating other female journalists who spoke in high voices. The 1996 *Daily Yomiuri* article (written by Muranaka) recounts that female newscasters with a low voice pitch were never encouraged by supervisors to actively pursue such a voice modulation.

The 1995 *New York Times* article touched upon a specific case in which a deep voiced announcer eventually acquired a newscaster's position at a prestigious broadcasting station. The *Daily Yomiuri* article is a continuation of the story of the phenomenon that the voices of female announcers are becoming deeper and provides further information about the importance of voice pitch for women in broadcasting. According to the article, there is a trend for female announcers to use a lower pitch. As evidence, the article cites the views of Kasuya at Utsunomiya University in Japan, who confirmed the trend by acoustic analyses. Kasuya deplores that female announcers at times unintentionally sound unpleasant to the listeners in their attempts to speak in deeper voices. He elaborates his opinion by comparing the human voice to a string instrument. He states that a violin and viola have different ranges of sounds which best suit each instrument. While it is possible to play viola tones by tuning violin strings, it would sound mediocre due to less tension on the strings. This is how a voice sounds when someone tries to speak in an unnaturally low voice. Kasuya apparently does not think that a women's low voice is as desirable as many people believe.

One of the newscasters whose voice was used in Kasuya's studies knows how hard it is to consciously control her voice. She feels that her natural voice usually resonates around the nose and mouth. However, when lowering her voice tone, she feels her vocal cords being strained. Kobayashi, The head of the NHK (Japan National Broadcasting Association) Communications Training Center, which trains announcers at the network, is also concerned about the trend. He explains that they never train their announcers to speak in a low voice. Moreover, an experienced announcer at TV Asahi comments that a low-pitched voice can make a news program appear 'heavier.' This applies even to cheerful pieces, when they are read in a low voice. The TV Asahi announcer stresses the need for announcers to acquire a wide range of voices and to deliver stories in appropriate tones and intonations according to content. Kobayashi also explains the importance of intonation when speaking with a lower voice. Apparently female voice professionals need to use larger intonation patterns when using a low voice just so that they would not sound like they are reading out of mantras.

The United States

Excerpts of the etiquette books and handbooks used in this section of the chapter to describe how American men and women were advised to speak were derived from numerous sources published in the nineteenth- and twentieth centuries. In 1975, Kramer (1975a) collected quotations from etiquette books and handbooks desirable and undesirable women's speech in general. I focus on the descriptions and prescriptions of American women's voice pitch found in such books. Beginning with *Culture and Dress of the Best American Society* published in 1800 until the 1959 *The Announcer's Handbook*, I found that American women's high-pitched voice was constantly discouraged.

In the chapter of 'Conversation' under 'Modulation,' *Culture and Dress of the Best American Society* (by Wells) advises:

> There is certain distinct but subdued tone of voice which is
> peculiar to only well-bred persons. A loud voice is both disagree-
> able and vulgar. It is better to err by the use of low than too loud a
> tone. (Wells, 1800: 67)

Under 'A Low Voice' in the same chapter, the book also conveys a further message aimed only at women:

> I think one can always tell a lady by her voice and laugh – neither
> of which ever be loud or coarse, but soft, low, and nicely modu-
> lated. Shakespeare's unfailing taste tells us that –
>
> 'A low voice is an excellent thing in woman.'
>
> And we believe that the habit of never raising the voice would
> tend much to the comfort and happiness of many at home: as a
> proof of good breeding, it is unfailing. (Wells, 1800: 71)

In *Etiquette For Ladies, With Hints on the Preservation, Improve-ment, and Display of Female Beauty* published in 1838 and 1841, there are teachings with regard to suppressing and modifying high-pitched loud voices.

> The low key belongs to the sullen, sulky, obstinate; the shrill note
> to the petulant, the pert, the impatient: some will pronounce the
> common question 'how do you do?' with such harshness and
> asperity, that they seem positively angry with you that should
> ever *do* at all. (1841: 175)
>
> Should she have too quick or encumbered an articulation, she
> ought to read with extreme slowness for several hours in the day,
> and even pay attention, in speaking, to check the rapidity or

confusion of her utterance. By similar antidotal means, she must
attack a propensity of talking in a high key. Better err in the
opposite extreme while she is prosecuting her cure, as the voice
will gradually and imperceptibly attain its most harmonious pitch,
than by at first attempting the medium, most likely retain too
much of the screaming key. A clear articulation, a tempered
intonation, and in a moderate key, are essentials in the voice of an
accomplished female. (1841: 184–5)

In *Better Than Beauty: A Guide to Charm* (1938), women are criticized for using a 'shrill' voice and advised to modulate their voices. In
the section of 'Your Tone of Voice' the guidebook states:

Many a woman is attractive until she talks. Then shrill voice or
nasal twang or deadly drawl may completely spoil the picture …
Your voice is worth working with. People are repelled, sometimes
consciously, sometimes unconsciously by an unpleasant voice.
And who can estimate the aura of charm which is induced by a
well-modulated voice? (Valentine and Thompson, 1938: 92–3)

In a 1950s handbook for broadcasters, women are criticized for their
high pitch:

often the higher-pitched female voices could not hold listener's
attention for any length of time, … 'Women's delivery … is lacking
in the authority needed for convincing newscast.' (Henneke and
Dumit 1959: 19 cited in Key 1972)

In 1969, Mannes (cited in Kramer 1975b: 49) mentioned a broad-
caster explaining why in the United States television networks seldom
hired women as reporters . Apparently, 'as a whole, people don't like to
hear women's voices telling them serious things' (Kramer, 1975b: 49).

Furthermore, in the 1957 *Handbook of Speech Pathology*, men's high-
pitched voice is viewed as clinically abnormal. American men who use
a higher-pitched voice have been and continue to be stigmatized and
labeled as impaired. In this handbook, Moore wrote with regard to the
relationship obtaining between high-pitched voice and masculinity as
follows:

A consistently high-pitched voice in the late adolescent and adult
male is of the most distressing of voice defects. The resemblance
to the female voice suggests a lack of masculinity. It is this
implication, with its psychosocial sequelae, which creates the
seriousness of the disorder, since the voice proper does not
interfere with communication; nor would it be unpleasant if it
were produced by a female (Moore, 1957: 658).

These facts indicate that many American women and some men have indeed spoken with high-pitched voices. They also reveal that the high-pitched voice utilized by both men and women has been generally stigmatized in American society.

Impressionistic Comments by Scholars

In this section, I will review previous observations of voice characteristics of both American and Japanese men and women made by researchers in various fields. These descriptions help us understand which particular voice pitch characteristics have influenced people's overall impressions about men and women's speech styles. However, they are only impressionistic in nature rather than based on empirical data.

Japan

Ernest Richard Edwards in his 1903 Etude *Phonetique de la Langue Japonaise* is responsible for making the earliest impressionistic remarks on Japanese women's voice characteristics. Edwards observed a tendency in Japanese women's language to exaggerate the stress and tone of words in order to emphasize their meanings. Edwards, having been a European scholar, also noticed the similar propensity among French and English women's linguistic behaviors of his time as below:

> Une autre tendance qu'on remarque dans le langage des
> Japonaises est assez repandue parmi les femmes francaises et
> anglaises. C'est l'employ excessif des mots intesifs, et
> l'exagération de l'accent de force et de l'intonation pour marque le
> renforcement. (Edwards, 1903: 79)

> Another tendency that has been noted in the language of
> Japanese women has been equally observed among French and
> English women. These women excessively employ exaggerated
> words as well as intonation which intensify the meanings of the
> words. (My translation from Edwards, 1969 in Japanese)

The content of the book, originally written in French, was translated into Japanese in 1935 and published in 1969. Referring to the overall brightness of the tone color/quality of the Japanese sounds, Edwards noted that the tune of the words of this language is high and the heightening of tone is widely used by the speakers (Edwards, 1969: 131). One of the tendencies that Edwards observed in Japanese women's language is that they exaggerate the stress and tone of the words in order to emphasize their meanings, as also seen among French and English women's linguistic behaviors (Edwards, 1969: 134). Japanese women utilize honorific prefixes such as [o-], [go-], [mi-] far more frequently than Japanese men do. In addition, they also often begin their sentences with such exclamatory expressions as [oja oja]('oh, dear'), [ma: ma:]('oh, my') (Edwards, 1969: 135).

In the 1960s and 1970s, six decades after Edward's observations, such researchers as Austin, Miller, Seward, Mashimo, and Libra presented their views pertaining to Japanese men's and women's voice pitch attributes. Austin and Seward agreed that Japanese men whom they had observed spoke loudly in an emphatically deep-voiced, 'rough' style of speaking. They found that Japanese women's voices, by contrast, emphasize femininity.

In 1965, Austin (1965: 38) noted striking linguistic differences between male and female speech as well as marked paralinguistic differences in Japan. He reported that Japanese women spoke with soft and high voices (almost a 'squeak'). Austin also remarked that Japanese men spoke loudly in low tones in Samurai movies – their speech sounded almost like a bark (Austin, 1965: 38). In 1968, Seward observed Japanese men's effort to emphasize the masculinity of their speech through their use of a deep-voiced, rough style of speaking. Austere faces and rigid postures often accompanied this. Seward believed that the speech and behaviors of Toshiro Mifune, which epitomized unbridled masculinity for Kurosawa's Samurai films, represented this style (Seward, 1968: 111). Miller (289) observed in 1967 that in situations where Japanese women were expected to be polite, they were very loquacious, ornamental and feminine in their *speech*. Mashimo (1969), while he extols the beauty of Japanese women's voice quality (which includes high-pitchedness), deplores the tendency of Japanese women to emphasize intonational variations. The following is my translation of his remarks. It appears that Mashimo's commentaries are based on the content reported in an issue of *Kotoba no Kenkyu* (Language Research Room) by NHK (Japan National Broadcasting Association). However, he did not provide full information of this reference.

> It is normal that men's voice pitch is low and women's high. The
> high pitch is the most striking characteristic of women's voice
> (Mashimo, 1969: 29–30). Women's voice is high-pitched. If men
> attempt to vocalize with the same pitch level as women's, their

vocal cords need to be unnaturally stretched. The manner of talking by female impersonators in theatrical performances and *rokyoku* (a story-telling performing art with musical accompaniment) performances is the example. (Mashimo, 1969: 30)

Vocal cords of youth are moist and tight. Therefore, their voice sounds bouncy and resonates high and cheerfully. Boys experience a period of voice change due to physiological reasons in their youth. However, girls do not go through this process and continued to be blessed with excellent voice quality for a long period (Mashimo, 1969: 33). Young women are truly blessed with good voice because of the type of vocal cords they are equipped with. Their voice is elastic, pretty, soft, clear, and full. At times, I even become totally enchanted when hearing their conversations in commuter trains. Many young women possess excellent voices. Their voice sounds like crystals rolling on the icy surface. I cannot find the equally delicate description for men's voice as theirs differs in quality. At any rate, I think that young Japanese women's voice in general is beautiful (Mashimo, 1969: 37). The beauty of women's voice that I praise is not limited to young women. I think that the beauty continues as they add years. Young maidens' clear and innocent voice as well as elderly ladies' soft voice are appropriately beautiful for their ages and even exhibit their personalities. (Mashimo, 1969: 35–6)

Furthermore, Mashimo noted an increased use of a greater range of pitch with contrasting pitch patterns among young Japanese women. He deplored the fact that these women sounded excessively emotional and asserted that such vocal features were unpleasant to the ear (Mashimo, 1969: 41–3).

Finally, Lebra in 1976 pointed out that in Japan, being a woman, implied assuming a woman's role with respect to others. Femininity thus may be consciously or deliberately displayed in dress as well as behavior and *speech* (Lebra, 1976: 87).

Emphasis on ultimate masculinity and femininity in Japanese men's and women's voice use is apparent in these comments. It should be noted, however, that I could not find any commentary made by Japanese scholars which vilifies high-pitched voice used by either Japanese women or Japanese men. In fact, Mashimo even remarked in neutral terms on the existence of a form of performing arts in which male players are expected to speak with high-pitched voices in Japan.

The United States

Darwin back in 1871 commented that the males among the lower animals almost always produce loud voices at the breeding season. He subsequently came to the conclusion that vocal organs of the human males may have inherited this trait following many generations of using loud voices frequently during excitement of love, jealousy, and rage. However, Ellis, in 1929, mentioned that Darwin's conclusion involving the inheritance of acquired traits is not universally supported (Ellis, 1929: 103). Ellis consequently presented a counter example by stating that females are more accomplished than males in voice usage. He introduced Monroe's 1903 finding that American girls at all ages possess larger singing ranges and boys[1] (Ellis, 1929: 104).

The earliest commentary made on American women which I found was that by Howells in *Harper's Bazaar* magazine in 1906 (although there exists an intriguing but controversial remark made on prostitutes' voice pitch by Masini in 1893 Italy).[2] In 1906, Howells criticized American women for having 'shrill' and 'not beautiful' voice. He believed that American women's speech was unpleasant despite their general supremacy over other women in the world at that time.

> The American woman was in the superiority to all other women ...
> And without doubt she had the sweetest voice in the world, ... but
> she had not always thought how to use it in her daily speech. For
> this reason alone she sometimes spoke through her nose, she
> twanged, she whittled, she snuffled, she whined, she whinnied the
> brilliant things which she was always incontestably saying.
> (Howells, 1906: 930)

Drawing on what E. R. Edwards' *Etude Phonetique de la Langue Japonaise*, mentioned above, Jespersen commented in 1922:

> Another tendency noticed in the language of Japanese women is
> pretty widely spread among French and English women, namely,
> the excessive use of intensive words and the exaggeration of
> stress and tone-accent to mark emphasis. (Jespersen, 1922: 243;
> compare to Edwards, 1903: 79)

Ellis, in 1929, described sexual vocal differences in terms of Darwin's evolutionary theory. Ellis notes that among most animals the female has a shriller and weaker voice than the male. He also refers to what he considers to be a well-known fact that a man's low voice and a woman's gentler but higher pitched voice have an impact on increasing pleasure during sexual intercourses. (Ellis, 1929: 104)

> This sexual vocal difference is by no means peculiar to Man: in
> most animals the female has a shriller and weaker voice than the
> male, as the hen, bitch, and mare, (Ellis, 1929: 104)

> That deeper voice of a man, the gentler but higher-pitched voice
> in woman, have their effect in heightening the pleasure of the
> sexes in each other's person in well known. (Ellis, 1929: 104)

In the 1960s and 1970s, American as well as English linguists fundamentally shared a common view that the use of a relatively 'wide pitch range with frequent and rapid long glides' (McConnell-Ginet, 1978: 549) epitomizes a widely-held stereotype of feminine speech. Austin (1965: 37) characterized the female paralanguage of courtship as 'high, oral and giggling, and in its final stage accompanied by 'wide pitch and intensity variation'. When a male imitates female speech, he does it 'in a high, rapid way'(Austin's example of '*Yes dear, I'll be down in a minute*'). It was Crystal's impression that effeminacy in English is associated with a 'simpering' voice. This characteristic is reflected, for example, in the use of a wider-than-normal pitch range (for men), frequently used complex tones, and occasional movement into a higher (falsetto) register (Crystal, 1971: 189).

> Intuitive impressions of effeminacy in English, for example, partly
> correct with segmental effects such as lisping, but are mainly non-
> segmental: a 'simpering' voice, for instance, largely reduces to the
> use of a wider pitch-range than normal (for men), with glissando
> effects between stressed syllables, a more frequent use of com-
> plex tones (e.g., the fall-rise and the rise-fall), the use of
> breathiness and huskiness in the voice. (Crystal, 1971: 189)

Although she did not disparage female speech, McConnell-Ginet (1978: 549) informally remarked that the use of a relatively 'wide pitch range with frequent and rapid long glides' symbolizes a widely-held stereotype of feminine speech. She made her observations based on the fact that when males imitate female speech, they highlight intonational contours with prominent and rapid pitch shifts. She further pointed out that only the female intonation patterns, *not the male ones*, are mocked in a derogatory manner (McConnell-Ginet, 1978: 549–50).

In addition, both Key and Kramer reported women's high-pitched voice as being associated with the undesirable trait of timidity and thus lacking in persuasive authority.

> It is quite likely that women use patterns of uncertainty and
> indefiniteness more often than men – patterns of 'PLIGHT'. (Key,
> 1972: 18)

> One of Key's students, in a brief exploratory experiment, listened to children in the 3rd, 4th, and 5th grades retell a story. 'The girls spoke with very expressive intonation, and the boys toned down the intonational features, even to the point of monotony, "playing it cool"' (Key, 1972: 18)

> Radio and TV broadcasters are concerned with pronunciation features; one handbook for announcers concluded that women's delivery 'is lacking in the authority needed for a convincing newscast' (Key, 1972: 18–19). However, in Germany and in the South, women's voices are heard frequently on the air.

> The pitch of the female voice, which is usually high-pitched because of the given physical traits of the vocal cords, is associated with the undesirable trait of timidness. (Kramer, 1775b: 49)

Interestingly, in the 1960s Austin, Luchsinger, and Arnold noted American women's desire to speak on a lower pitch level than they had employed previously.

Low pitch has lately become fashionable for women, but fifty years

> ago all 'ladies' spoke with a high pitch. (Austin, 1965: 37)

> Many American women, on the other hand, find it desirable to speak on an artificially low pitch level. Laryngologists are occasionally asked by middle-aged women how they might lower their speaking voices because the normal speech range of the soprano sounds unpleasantly 'screechy' to them. (Luchsinger and Arnold, 1965: 100)

The general tendency of the remarks made on American men and women's voice characteristics by these scholars is that high-pitched voices (with or without variable intonation patterns) utilized by women are negatively perceived. The lack of statements made on American men's voice may indicate that their average voice is regarded as standard, thus unproblematic.

Notes

1. Monroe, W. (1903) *Psychological Review*. March, 155. This Monroe's article could not be found as cited by Ellis.
2. When he measured prostitutes' larynx and vocal cords, Masini discovered that 29 out of his 50 prostitute subjects possessed larger larynx and vocal cords as well as slightly masculine voice mixed with both high and low pitches (Masini 1893: 145).

2　Acoustic Analyses of Voice Pitch

Early acoustic phonetic investigations of voice pitch initiated in the early twentieth century in both the US and Japan yielded results consistent with the impressionistic remarks on men's and women's voice pitches made earlier. That is, men's voice pitch is lower than that of women; there is a considerable gap between the voice ranges of the two groups. More recent acoustic phonetic research, however, reconsidered the previous findings, which basically agreed for the impressionistic accounts made on men's and women's voice pitches. The investigators of these researches mainly utilized vowel sounds, passages, and constructed (instructed) dialogues as their speech data. This chapter includes a review of most investigations conducted thus far in Japan and the US. The review will be divided into two sections: a section describing studies conducted prior to 1980 followed by a section recounting those performed after 1980. The focus will be on the investigations of the voice pitch of relatively young adult men and women (ranging in age between 17 and 39). In addition, the review will extend to some studies of middle-aged or elderly speakers as long as these studies also include speakers in the younger age range (of 17 ~ 39).

Both psychologists and linguists have long attempted to establish the relationship obtaining between types of emotions and prosodic features. By the end of the twentieth century most researchers had come to consensus that there was some correlation. The chapter highlights the most consistent correlations that have been found between increases in mean voice pitch, pitch range, and pitch variability of speech and types of emotion labeled as 'elation' reported in all studies. In addition, it has been reported that vocal of emotions portrayals produced in one language can be recognized by speakers of *other* languages with better-than-chance accuracy.

Early Analyses

Japan

In Japan, acoustic analyses of men's and women's voice pitch have only been conducted sporadically in the past. The speech data utilized for these investigations derived from passages read by informants as well as demonstration by them of vowel sounds articulated for several seconds of time. Although the procedures and devices adopted for these examinations varied considerably, in terms of Hertz values on the linear scale, it was shown that there was a significant *gap* between male and female voice pitch ranges. This section of the chapter herein presents studies by Kanetsune (1938), Kasuya (reported in Muranaka, 1996), Terasawa, Kakita, and Hirano (1984), and Tsuge, Kakami, and Fukaya (1987).

Kanetsune (1938)

In 1938 Kanetsune examined speech samples derived from a Japanese man and woman, who were asked to articulate words and phrases as if they were truly conversing. He apparently used a type of oscillograph[1] for measuring these subjects' voice pitch in terms of Hertz (on linear-scale). However, he did not specify which particular types of microphone and oscillograph were utilized for the investigation.

Kanetsune observed that the rate of pitch modulation tended to increase and the fundamental frequency range was inclined to widen in expressive words and phrases. He found that Japanese men and women differed considerably with regard to frequency modulation when they uttered the same words and phrases. The voice pitch range of men was 76 Hz~400 Hz as compared to 94 Hz~620 Hz for women. In my opinion, Kanetsune's measurement of 94 Hz for the female's lowest voice pitch is either a measurement error or an incident of creaky voice.[2] Moreover, the 620 Hz measurement of the female's highest voice pitch appears to be exceedingly high.

Kanetsune also examined the female informant conversing with a friend over the telephone. However, he could not recognize most of their utterances as he could not identify the locations of consonants and vowels. As a result, he was only able to detect greetings and set phrases articulated by these informants. Kanetsu reasoned that these expressions were perhaps produced as if the informants were reading passages.

Kanetsune's references include several research studies on experimental phonetics documented in his time. However, the information he provided for each study was incomplete.[3]

Kasuya,[4] Suzuki, and Kido (1968)

In 1968 Kasuya obtained the average voice pitch of eight adult male and female speakers (four in each sex) in their 20s for his experiment. The informants used for his study were all university students. These informants were instructed to articulate for several seconds the five basic vowels of /a/, /e/, /i/, /o/, and /u/ as naturally as possible. The software utilized for measurement was Sound Spectrograph SG-04A (manufactured by Lion). The number of speech samples collected was 85 (/i/), 92 (/e/), 85 (/a/), 81 (/o/), and 90 (/u/) respectively. The average voice pitch of these informants ranged from 108 Hz to 133 Hz for the males and spanned between 218 Hz and 230 Hz for the females.[5]

Terasawa, Kakita, and Hirano (1984)

One of the acoustic features which Terasawa, Kakita, and Hirano measured in 1984 was fundamental frequency during habitual phonation. They examined the voices of two groups of male and female speakers (30 in each group, 60 total). One group ranged in age between 22 and 39, while the other ranged in age between 19 and 31. The researchers do not indicate the specific kind of speech data which they elicited from the informants. They explain that the informants were asked to articulate their voices for a few seconds after breathing normally for a while. For the males the average F0 was 121 Hz and the F0 range spanned between 85 Hz and 164 Hz. The female mean F0 was 238 Hz and their F0 range extended from 205Hz to 277 Hz.

Tsuge, Kakami, and Fukaya (1987)

In 1987, Tsuge, Kakami, and Fukaya reported a study exploring the possible link between height, weight and fundamental frequency of Japanese vowels and /e:/. Their subjects were 92 males and 22 females studying in a School of Dentistry (at Aichi-Gakuin University), whose ages ranged between 22 and 28. They found a correlation between female speakers' height, weight, and vowel pitch frequency. The researchers, however, found no association between male speakers' height, weight, and vowel pitch frequency.

The subjects were first asked to pronounce the five basic vowels in the combinations of /a, i, u, e, o/, /o, e, u, i, a/, and /i, e, a, o, u, u, o, a, e, i/ twice respectively. Then, they were instructed to read a constructed conversational sentence containing, a long vowel, /e:/, which functions as discourse filler in Japanese. The investigators extracted this elongated vowel /e:/ and measured its fundamental frequency for each subject. They apparently chose this vowel in the hope that it would represent a relatively spontaneous utterance.

Tsuge, Kakami, and Fukaya employed Sound Spectrograph (manufactured by Lyon SG – 09) to measure the fundamental frequency of these vowels. The mean fundamental frequency of five vowels for male subjects was 129 Hz, ranging between 97 Hz and 163 Hz. The mean for female subjects was 225 Hz, with a range between 205 Hz and 239 Hz. Fundamental frequency of the vowel /e:/ spanned from 99 Hz to 162 Hz for the males and 190 Hz and 247 Hz for the females. It was noted that the mean frequency of this vowel for male subjects was lower than that of the five vowels by 3.5 Hz. For female subjects the difference was 1.7 Hz higher for this vowel than that for the five vowels.

In 1980 Honjo and Isshiki conducted phoniatric and laryngoscopic examinations[6] in order to determine both voice and laryngeal characteristics of aged men and women. It will not be included here, however, because it did not include a comparative younger age group. I have also chosen not to discuss another study that Kitajima published in 1973 concerning very slight pitch perturbation of sustained vowels articulated by normal Japanese speakers.

The United States

American speech researchers performed a considerable number of experiments measuring men's and women's voice pitch in the past. Numerous investigations on voice pitch of American men and women of various ages were conducted starting from the 1920s. All of the early experiments adopted passages read by informants and produced similar results revealing that men's and women's voice pitch ranges did not in fact overlap (in terms of Hz values). As was the case in early acoustic analyses conducted in Japan, the methodologies of these examinations employed by American linguists differ significantly. Researches adduced here include those of Weaver (1924), Cowan (1936), Provonost (1942), Snidercor (1943 and 1951), Mysak (1959), McGlone and Hollien. (1963), Terango (1966), Saxman and Burke (1967), Fitch and Holbrook (1970), Hollian and Shipp (1972), Hollien and Jackson (1973), Linke (1973), and Stoicheff (1981).

Weaver (1924)

In 1924, Weaver measured average voice pitch levels of 43 young university students (20 females and 23 males) using the apparatus called, the 'phonautograph.'[7] It was designed and constructed by Weaver and his collaborator in the psychological laboratory at the University of Wisconsin (25). The subjects were students in an elementary speech class at the same university whose training in vocal expression and music was substantially uniform. They were asked to speak the selected words from the poem (Austin Dobson's dialogue in verse, '*Tu Quoque*') into the recorder in such a manner as to express all possible meaning (36). Weaver obtained an average value of 318 Hz for the female subjects and 151 Hz for the male subjects. Moreover, he found that with the exception of the first subject among the men, the pitch registers of the two groups were mutually exclusive. As for the amount of inflectional modulation, it was found that the area of the melody curve of the women was nearly twice as that of the men in terms of Hertz on the linear scale. On the logarithmic scale, the difference was reduced.[8]

Cowan (1936)

Ten contemporary actors and actresses who were playing in New York during the 1934–5 season participated in Cowan's 1936 study. The speakers and selections of speech included Kenneth MacKenna's valedictorian address from *Merrily We Roll Along* by Kaufman and Hart and Margaret Wycherly's monologue from *Candida* by George Bernard Shaw. Fourteen recordings were selected from the wide range of different kinds of dramatic speech obtained using high quality phonograph records for analysis. The analysis utilized phonophotographic apparatus[9] and technique in the phonetics laboratories of the (State) University of Iowa. Cowan obtained 20,000 measurements of average pitch, intensity and approximately 215,000 individual sound waves. The average median pitch level for all male voices was 141 Hz, ranging between 134 Hz and 146 Hz. The average median pitch level of all female voices was 233 Hz, ranging from 199 Hz to 295 H.

Provonost (1942)

Provonost's (1942) subjects were male students who were recommended for their superior voices by the staff members of the Department of Speech at the (State) University of Iowa. According to Fairbanks, Superior speakers are assumed to 'approach the use of pitch levels which permit their mechanisms to function of the voices maximum general efficiency in speech' (Fairbanks 1940: 112–13). The best four readings of Fairbanks' 'Rainbow Passage'[10] read by these subjects were selected by seven trained observers. Provonost then computed the phonograph recordings of each reading through the phonophotographic technique of sound wave analysis (described in Cowan) and obtained fundamental frequency measurements. The results of his investigation of the male speaking pitch levels showed that mean fundamental frequency was 132.1 Hz.

Snidercor 1943

The subjects used in Snidercor's 1943 investigation were the same as those selected in Provonost's 1939 and 1942 research studies. They were male students of speech at the (State) University of Iowa. Snidercore derived comparative data from impromptu speech. He first recorded in a sound proof room each of six subjects' delivering a speech on the topic of 'My Future Job' in approximately one minute. One week later, the subjects were asked to read typewritten texts of their original speeches in the same experimental condition. Snidercor utilized the phonophotographic technique (described in Cowan) for his study. Median pitch levels were 120 Hz for improvised speech reading and 129 Hz for passage reading. As for mean pitch levels, it was 120 Hz for impromptu speech reading and 132 Hz for passage reading. Snidecore also found that higher pitch levels and increased pitch variations were observed in passage reading than impromptu speech reading when a scripted originally impromptu speech was read.

Snidercor (1951)

In 1951, Snidercor examined the pitch and duration characteristics of the voices of superior female speakers reading factual material. The subjects were assumed to be speech students at the (State) University of Iowa as he noted that their selection procedure was identical to that used by Provonost in 1942. Snidercor compared these data with previously found values for superior male speakers. The reading material used for this investigation was Fairbanks' 'Rainbow Passage'. Twenty-five adult female subjects were selected for their superior general effectiveness in speech and voice usage. From this group, eight subjects who demonstrated the most superior voice usage were selected. Snidecore made phonograph recordings of the passage for each subject in a sound proof room. After 14 trained observers compared each reading twice, the six recordings ranked highest were selected for measurement of fundamental frequency. The phonophotographic technique used for voice pitch analysis was that described in Cowan. Snidercor obtained an average median pitch level of 212 Hz for the speech samples.

Mysak (1959)/McGlone and Hollien (1963)

In 1959, Mysak examined median voice pitch of 39 older male subjects from the four institutions for the aged and also from private homes in Lafayette, Indiana. The older group consisted of 12 individuals in the age group from 65 to 79 years. Mysak's study included a sample of the age group ranging in age from 32 to 62 years. The result of this group, however, is not contained in Table 2 as the age range is too wide for comparison with the outcomes of other studies which focused on relatively young speaker pools. In 1963 McGlone and Hollien obtained mean voice pitch of the aged women (between 65 and 94 years) and compared the results with similar data reported for females of other ages. Their subjects were 21 advanced aged women selected from a large number of volunteers residing at the Kansas Masonic Home in Wichita. However, I cannot use the results of this investigation in my aggregate data table (Table 2), since it did not include comparative speech samples from younger age groups.

Terango (1966)

In 1966 Terango measured voice pitch of 40 American males, 20 of whom were thought to have effeminate voices and 20, masculine voices at Kent State University, Ohio. Each subject read the 98-word first paragraph of the Fairbanks' 'Rainbow Passage' in a sound treated room. The pitch of 55 words out of this paragraph was measured by the phonophotographic technique described in Cowan. The speech samples were rated by 146 listeners (27 male and 117 female college students) for confirmation of their effeminate and masculine voice qualities.

Terango then compared his results with those derived from studies conducted on male voice pitch prior to his. The findings revealed that the median pitch of American males considered to possess 'effeminate' voices (127 Hz) was not in fact higher than the median or mean pitch of American males reported in two other comparable previous studies (133 Hz in Phihour's study in 1948 and 132 Hz in McIntosh's 1939 investigation, cited in Terango) of male speaking voice pitch. Moreover, in my observation, the median pitch of males who had been judged as possessing 'masculine' voices was considerably *lower* than the mean pitch of Polish males later reported by Majewski, Hollien, and Zalewski. The median pitch of American males whose voices were regard masculine was 100 Hz, the median pitch of Polish men was 137.6 Hz (Terango 1966: 592; Majewski, Hollien, and Zalewski 1972: 121).

Saxman and Burke (1967)

The Speakers for Saxman's 1967 study on middle-aged women's voice pitch included nine women who were between 30 and 40 years of age with a median age of 33.5 years. Each subject was instructed to read the first paragraph of the 'Rainbow Passage' in the acoustic chamber of the Perdue University Speech Science Laboratory. An Ampex 601 magnetic tape recorder and an associated directional microphone of the same high quality were used for recording. Mean fundamental frequency and standard deviation of fundamental frequency were analyzed by means of the Fundamental Frequency Indicator (FFI),[11] a digital readout of F0 tracking device described in Hollien and Paul (1969). Mean speaking fundamental frequency of these (30 to 40 year old) women was 196.34 Hz, ranging from 171.18 Hz to 221.75 Hz.

Fitch and Holbrook (1970)

In 1970, Fitch and Holbrook obtained recordings of 200 students of the Florida State University (100 males and 100 females) who were judged to have normal speech, voice, and hearing by three judges holding the American Speech and Hearing Association Certificate of clinical competence. Their ages ranged between 17.5 and 25.5 years. The speech sample collected in a soundproof booth from these subjects was the middle 55 words of 'Rainbow Passage' by Fairbanks. Fitch and Holbrook employed a device called FLORIDA (Frequency Lowering Or Raising Intensity Determining Apparatus) to locate modal voice fundamental frequency. It was found that the mean of the vocal fundamental frequencies of the males was 116.65 Hz and that of the females was 217 Hz.

Hollien and Shipp (1972)

In 1972, Hollien and Shipp compared mean speaking fundamental frequencies of 175 male speakers whose ages ranged between 20 and 89 years. These subjects were grouped into age decades, each consisting of 25 subjects. Hollien and Shipp derived the speech data from having the subjects read the 'Rainbow Passage.' They acquired mean fundamental frequency measures of each subject using the Fundamental

Frequency Indicator (FFI). The result shows that the mean speaking fundamental frequency for the 20 to 29-year-old group was 119.5 Hz while the value obtained for the 30–39 year olds was 112.2 Hz.

Hollien and Jackson (1973)

In 1973, Hollien and Jackson reported research focusing on the speaking fundamental frequency and related characteristics of 157 male students' voices, whose ages ranged between 17.9 and 25.8 years (mean = 20.3). The subjects were students at the University of Florida, who were also speakers of Southern region dialect and had no history of extensive voice training for laryngeal pathology. The subjects first read a prose passage, R. L. Stephenson's *Apology for Idlers*, approximately three minutes in length. Subjects then gave three-minute-talks on one of four topics, including: 'what I like to do most on vacation'; 'the most interesting thing that has ever happened to me'; 'my favorite sports'; 'what's I like best about my program of study.'

Hollien and Jackson utilized an Ampex tape recorder for recordings the speech. They then edited and analyzed the resultant taped speech samples using the Fundamental Frequency Indicator (FFI). It was found that a mean oral reading fundamental frequency for passage reading was 129.4 Hz whereas that for extemporaneous speaking was 123.3 Hz.

Linke (1973)

In 1973, Linke analyzed the voices of 27 young adult females selected for their general effectiveness of voice usage based on ratings made by a panel of 38 judges in speech and speech pathology at the (State) University of Iowa. It appears that these speakers read the 'Rainbow Passage' although it was not precisely indicated but only implied. Linke measured frequency range and variability using a photophonellegraphic[12] technique, and then correlated the values with ratings of vocal effectiveness. He found that his subjects employed slightly lower average median frequency levels (201 Hz) than the levels found in previous studies for female voices. Their median frequency levels were located at the lower end of their overall voice ranges, as compared to male voices previously analyzed. Linke also discovered smaller measures of pitch range in his female subjects than their male counterparts, as measured in previous investigations. Moreover, Linke's study showed smaller frequency variability than superior female speakers, in Scidecor's 1940 study, particularly the data derived from the 90 percent range (as opposed to the total range). He concluded that female speakers judged to have effective voices appear to demonstrate less variability in pitch usage than do corresponding groups of males during oral reading.

With regard to the correlation with ratings of general speaking effectiveness, neither median frequency levels nor standard deviations computed on the total voice pitch range showed a significant relation, according to Linke. Linke speculated that American women in general might be utilizing pitch levels which are lower than appropriate for the most effective usage of their voices in speaking.

Stoicheff (1981)

Stoicheff examined speaking fundamental frequency of 111 healthy adult females who had never smoked or who had ceased smoking 15 or more years before his study. These subjects' ages ranged from 20 to 82. Subjects within each age group were selected from various occupational groups such as secretaries, nurses, housewives, students, and so forth. They read the first paragraph of Fairbanks' 'Rainbow Passage' into a Beyer Dynamic (M69) unidirectional microphone with an Ampex AG-440B audio tape recorder in a sound-treated area. Stoicheff obtained mean fundamental frequency measurements using the Fundamental Frequency Indicator (FFI), located at the Communication Sciences Laboratory, University of Florida. She found that the mean fundamental frequency of the 21 speakers belonging to the 20–29 years age group was 224.3 Hz (192.2 Hz ~ 275.4 Hz). The corresponding figure for the 18 subjects belonging to the 30–39 years age group was 213.3 Hz (181 Hz ~ 240.6 Hz).

Kasuya (1996)

Previously mentioned Kasuya's studies included F0 measurements of an American female newscaster performed in 1991. In his 1991 study reported in 1996 the Daily Yomiuri article, nine US female newscasters, including some from CNN, were sampled for comparison. The average pitch of these US newscasters was 188 Hz. This was lower than the number reported for the Japanese counterparts in his 1995 study. Moreover, these US female newscasters spoke with a less marked intonation on the average than their Japanese counterparts did.

The nature of the aforementioned examinations is purely *acoustic* phonetic as opposed to *socio*-phonetic. These investigations fundamentally confirmed previous impressionistic observations of men's and women's voice pitch across nations and did not raise any socio-cultural or socio-political issues. Due to differing and incomparable research methodologies, acoustic apparatus, and data sets utilized in these studies, I found it essentially impossible to definitively describe any significant difference between Japanese and American voice pitches observed in these early investigations. However, the gap between men's and women's voice ranges across culture can be consistently observed.

More Recent Analyses

Post-1980s acoustic analyses concerning voice pitch began questioning both stereo-typical portrayals and earlier acoustical findings of men's and women's voice pitch. These analyses raised intriguing socio-cultural and socio-political issues pertaining to Japanese and American societies.

Japan

This part of the chapter initially presents Ohara's 1992 study on bilingual Japanese women and Kasuya's longitudinal studies in the 1990s on changes in Japanese female newscasters' voice pitch.

Ohara (1992)

In her study of bilingual Japanese men and women, Ohara discovered that Japanese women adopted higher pitch on the average when speaking Japanese than in speaking English. She argued that this high pitch was chosen so as to approximate a particular vocal image reflecting socio-culturally-desired personal attributes and social role.

Her subjects were six female and six male native speakers of Japanese who were students at the University of Hawaii at Manoa. The female subjects' ages ranged between 22 to 29 and the males' 21 and 31. They were asked to read ten English sentences taken from the chapter in the linguistics course book written in English as well as ten Japanese sentences, which were translation of the ten English sentences. Ohara recorded the speech samples in the phonetics laboratory at the University of Hawaii at Manoa. Each subject's fundamental frequency was measured using Visi Pitch manufactured by Kay Elemetrics Corp.

Ohara found that female subject employed 19 Hz to 48 Hz higher pitch when they speak Japanese compared to the pitch they utilized when speaking English, with much larger pitch range than that in English. The overall pitch ranges in terms of average mean lowest and highest, which I computed from her data, are 152 Hz ~ 251.67 Hz for the females and 106.5 Hz ~ 150.33 Hz for the males. Ohara expected Japanese males to utilize low pitch when they spoke in Japanese. However, half of the male subjects adopted higher pitch and the other half lower pitch when speaking Japanese.

Kasuya (1996)

In Kasuya's two investigations, the average pitch of female Japanese announcers in 1995 decreased compared with those sampled in 1991. *The Daily Yomiuri* journalist, Muranaka, reported his studies on 13 June 1996. The studies were conducted by two of Kasuya's students at Utsunomiya University in Japan: Takao Sekine in 1991 and Akihisa Ono in 1995. They compared the 1991 recording of the voices of 11 newscasters and announcers (six from the Japan National Broadcasting Association) with the 1995 recording of the voices of ten newscasters (six from commercial networks). Four of the women sampled in both studies were the same. In the 1991 study, nine US female newscasters, including some from CNN, were sampled for comparison.

The average pitch of Japanese announcers in 1995 was 216 Hz, ranging between 191 Hz and 242 Hz, compared to 230 Hz, ranging between 198 Hz and 269 Hz in 1991. The average pitch of their US counterparts in 1991 was 188 Hz, still lower than the number reported in the latest Japanese study. As far as intonation (or rise and fall of voice pitches) was concerned, Japanese female newscasters spoke with a more marked intonation on average than their US counterparts did in 1991 and the difference became more conspicuous in 1995. The methodologies of these studies were not reported.

The United States

Ensuing discussions on voice pitch research conducted in America in the 1980s and 1990s by a British researcher, Henton (1989, 1995), are highlighted in this section of the chapter. Henton, by adopting the non-linear scale (semitones) of analysis, demonstrated that male and female pitch ranges examined prior to her own study were not significantly different. She also found no statistically significant difference in the pitch dynamism (variability) between the sexes of the speakers. The finding was in contradistinction to the previous characterizations of female intonation patterns noted in a wide variety of sources.

Before I delve into Henton's investigations, I would like to mention a tentative, but enlightening report on the results of a perception test of men's and women's voice pitch conducted in England in 1978. Olwen, inspired by Richards' remarks[13] on the discrepancies between acoustic measurements of voice pitch and the raters' auditory perception, performed a small-scale perception test.

Olwen (1978)

Olwen collected speech samples from 20 males and 20 females, all undergraduates or postgraduates at the University of Bristol, England. Speakers read three passages and answered two questions regarding each passage into the Uher 4000 apparatus. The data reported in Olwen's study was based on one of the 12 tapes initially produced, containing recordings of five male and five female speakers. Five male and five female raters were selected from the same sample population as the speakers.

The female speech samples were assessed as possessing higher pitch, but not greater range width or more rapid frequency of pitch changes than the male samples. This was true for all speech garnered from passage reading and question answering. The latter two findings were apparently not in agreement with the findings of the previously conducted acoustic analyses by Richards. According to Olwen, Richards discovered that the female speakers utilized a wider gliding pattern for upward and downward pitch movements with abrupt downward changes more frequently than males. By contrast, the male speakers adopted more abrupt upward changes and flat fundamental frequency than females did.

Henton (1989)

Olwen was cautious in presenting her results due to the small number of informants used as judges in her study. Henton (1989), on the other hand, had no reservations about questioning the validity of characterizing female speech in terms such as 'high-pitched,' 'shrill,' 'overemotional,' and 'swoopy.' She attempted to demonstrate that many such depictions of female pitch characteristics have stemmed from incorrect interpretations of the experimental measurements. She argued that these descriptions used for pitch attributes are more influenced by the speaker's social evaluations than by the actual auditory perception of the pitch itself.

Scholars claimed that the human ear responds to speech sounds logarithmically rather than linearly (e.g., Hudson and Holbrook, 1981; Graddol, 1986). Henton, therefore, adopted the non-linear scale (semitones[14]) of analysis and re-evaluated a large number of studies that reported pitch ranges of speaking fundamental frequency prior to her research. These previous studies which she re-assessed included not only different variations of the English language but also languages such as Polish and Swedish. The measurements of these studies were derived from various types of linguistic contexts: sustained vowels, reading passages, and constructed dialogues. She converted the measurements of pitch ranges reported in these studies into semitones. It was observed in her re-evaluation that the males generally had a greater pitch range than females did.

She then obtained new speech data in American English from ten socially homogeneous American informants (five males and five females). They were graduate students at the University of California, Davis or Berkeley. They read a set of two passages (one containing a large portion of nasal vowels, the other none) originally created for an unrelated research. Henton collected the speech samples using an Electro-Voice condenser microphone and a Sony TC-756-2 reel-to-reel tape recorder in a sound-treated room located in the Phonology Laboratory at the University of California, Berkeley. Pitch measurements were obtained using a Visi Pitch pitch meter (VP 6087 DS). She calculated pitch range for four standard deviations, including the 96 percent sample of her data, and then converted the Hertz measurements into semitones. The results indicated that pitch ranges used by males and females in her study were not significantly different in terms of semitones (1989: 307). Incidentally, the average voice pitch of Henton's subjects in terms of Hertz, which I calculated from her data, were 113.14 Hz (93.2 Hz ~125.1 Hz) for the males and 180.14 Hz (155.5 Hz ~ 215.1 Hz) for the females.

Henton argued that this lack of difference showed the inaccuracy of depictions of female speech as 'swoopy' and thus over-emotional (terms that are associated acoustically with wider pitch ranges). She further pointed out that these characterizations resulted from interpreters' androcentric attitudes, identifying women's speech as inferior to men's.

Henton (1995)

In 1995, Henton also examined pitch dynamism of female speakers. She defines pitch dynamism as 'the degree of rapidity of changes in a speaker's pitch range from high points to low points' (Henton, 1995: 44).

In this study, Henton utilized the same speech samples obtained for her 1989 investigation. Therefore, the procedure employed was identical to that of her previous study. However, pitch dynamism values for each subject were measured at the Linguistic Program, University of California, Santa Barbara.

In contradiction to the repeated characterizations of female intonation described as using a wide variety of pitch ranges, Henton found no statistically significant difference between the sex of the speakers and the pitch dynamism used by them. Henton, however, cited a study by Woods (1992), which utilized conversational speech data sets, stating that the result may differ if naturally occurring speech data were used.

Tables 2.1 and 2.2 summarize the aforementioned acoustical studies of voice pitch for each nation. The list of these relevant voice pitch investigations contained in these tables is considered to be nearly exhaustive ones for the American English and Japanese languages. Voice pitch research conducted on European languages is excluded from this table.

Table 2.1 Survey of previous acoustic phonetic studies of Japanese men's and women's voice pitch

Sources	Mean/Median F0 (F0 range)		Number of subjects	Age	Speech data type
	Male	Female			
Kanetsune (1938)	76 Hz~400 Hz	94 Hz~620 Hz	3 (1male/2 females)	relatively young	Reading words/phrases
Kasuya (1968)	121.75 Hz (108 Hz ~ 133 Hz)	224.75 Hz (218 Hz ~ 230 Hz)	8 (4 males/ 4 females)	22~26	Articulating Five basic vowels
Terasawa, Kakita, and Hirano (1984)	121 Hz (85 Hz ~ 164 Hz)	238 Hz (205Hz ~ 277 Hz)	60 (30 males/30 females)	22 ~39	Sustained voicing
Tsuge, Kakami, and Fukaya (1987)	129 Hz (97 Hz ~ 163 Hz)	225 Hz (205 Hz ~ 239 Hz)	114 (92 males/22 females)	22 ~ 28	Articulating Five basic vowels
	(99 Hz ~ 162 Hz)	(190 Hz ~ 247 Hz)	Same as above	Same as above	Sustained vowel [e:] occurring as a discourse filler
Ohara (1992)	(106.5 Hz ~ 150.33 Hz: mean lowest ~ mean highest)	(152 Hz ~ 251.67 Hz: mean lowest ~ mean highest)	12(6 males/ 6 females)	21 ~ 31	Reading sentences
Ohara (1999)	128Hz	261.6 Hz	10 (5 males/5 females)	26 ~ 36 (males) 26~ 42 (female)	Leaving phone message
Kasuya (1995)		1991: 230 Hz(198 Hz ~ 269 Hz) 1995: 216 Hz(191 Hz ~ 242 Hz)	4 females same 4 females	relatively young	Newscasting Newscasting

Table 2.2 Survey of previous acoustic phonetic studies of American men's and women's voice pitch

Sources	Mean/Median F0 (F0 range)		Number of subjects	Age	Speech data type
	Male	Female			
Weaver (1924)	151 Hz	318 Hz	43 (23 males/ 20 females)	College	Reading poem
Cowan (1936)	141 Hz (134 Hz ~146 Hz)	233 Hz (199 Hz ~ 295 Hz)	10	Unknown	Reading dramatic speech
Provonost (1942)	132.1 Hz		4 males	College	Reading passage
Snidercor (1943)	129 Hz		4 males	College	Reading passage
	120 Hz		4 males	College	Impromptu speech
Snidercor (1951)		212 Hz	6 females	College	Reading passage
Terango (1966)	100 Hz (masculine voices)		20 males	College	Reading passage
	127 Hz (effeminate voices)		20 males	College	Reading passage
Saxman & Burke (1967)		196.34 Hz (171 .18 Hz ~ 221.75 Hz)	9 females	30 ~ 40	
Fitch & Holbrook (1970)	116.65 Hz	217 Hz	200 (100males/ females)	College	
Hollian, and Shipp (1972)	119.5 Hz		25 males	20 ~ 29	Reading passage
	112.2 Hz		25 males	30 ~ 39	Reading passage
Hollien and Jackson (1973)	129.4 Hz		157 males	College	Reading passage
	123.3 Hz		157 males	College	Impromptu speech
Linke (1973)		201 Hz	27 females		Reading prose
Stoicheff (1981)		224.3 Hz (192.2 Hz ~ 275.4 Hz) 213.3 Hz (181 Hz ~ 240.6 Hz)	21 females 18 females	20-29 30-39	Reading passage
Henton (1989)	113.14 Hz (93.2 Hz ~125.1Hz)	180.14 Hz (155.5 Hz ~ 215.1 Hz)	10 (5 males/females)	23 ~ 37	Reading non-nasal passage
Kasuya (1996) (in Daily Yumiuri)		188 Hz	9 female newscasters	Unknown	News casting

Voice Pitch and Emotion Research

The United States and Japan

In America, various relations between speech and emotion or specific emotions have been investigated by a number of researchers. I, however, included only those research results that are most relevant to the main argument of this book.

Skinner is the researcher who initiated such research in 1935. He noticed that writers in his time had only subjectively evaluated the conditions known as 'joy' and 'sadness.' Skinner collected normal speech by evoking the desired type of emotion by natural (as opposed to artificial) simulation. He subsequently examined the data which were photographed with the oscillograph. The study used nine male and ten female subjects who all had considerable training and experience in speech or acting at the University of Wisconsin. Seven subjects were prominent in the profession of teaching speech.

Skinner's subjects read an excerpt of literature claimed by experts to most effectively induce the targeted states of emotions (Ina Coolbrith's 'In Blossom Time' for happiness and Eugene Field's 'Little Boy Blue' for sadness), while their voice was recorded. They then listened to two pieces of music (Strauss-Tausig's *One Lives But Once*, Part 2 to evoke happiness and Robert G. Ingersol's *A Vison of War* sadness), followed by vocalizing a vowel 'ah' which lasted for a few seconds. Finally, they were asked what mood or emotion they experienced while reading the literature and listening to the music.

Skinner also obtained the subjects' psychogalvanic[15] information in order to confirm that all subjects were affected emotionally. The study found that in the psychogalvanic reactions, the subjective accounts, the voice waves almost perfectly correlated with the stimuli which produced them. In the speech which had evoked happiness (joy), Skinner by and large detected substantially higher pitch of the voice than in the voice pitch associated with sad situations. He also found this difference was statistically significant for stimuli produced by both male and female speakers.

Two decades after the earliest studies by Skinner (1935), Pronovost (1939), and Fairbanks (1940), linguists and psychologists began finding some common correlations obtaining between voice cues and emotion types through utilization of speech synthesis or perception tests.

In 1960, Uldall applied 16 pitch contours to recordings of four sentences by synthesis. She then asked listeners to rate the patterns with respect to ten scales of attitude types such as Bored/Interested, etc. Uldall drew conclusions about several general features of the intonation patterns with respect to three factors: Pleasant/Unpleasant, Interest/Lack of Interest and Authoritative/Submissive. The listeners of the study had a tendency to rate yes-or-no question and question-word question synthesized with a wide voice pitch range as 'interested'. On the other hand, they were inclined to identify statement, yes-or-no question and question-word question generated in a narrow voice pitch range with 'lack of interest'.

Huttar in 1968 examined emotional states of normal speech by one adult male American collected without recourse to artificial simulation of emotions from a series of classroom lectures and discussions. Twelve subjects evaluated 30 utterances extracted from this speaker on nine seven-point scale semantic differential scales[16] for pitch, loudness, and speed.

Huttar measured minimum and maximum fundamental frequencies and maximum intensity as well as total duration of one of the tokens of these utterances by viewing spectrograms[17] and continuous amplitude displays. The results of Pearson's linear correlations coefficients suggest that both the fundamental frequency and intensity ranges increase in proportion to the increase in the degree of perceived emotional involvement of speech.

A German scholar, Scherer (1986) provides a summary of the studies investigating the correlations between types of emotion and acoustically measured prosodic features as well as those reporting the results of perception tests in which listeners identified types of emotion expressed by professional and lay actors. The summary includes the list of research conducted between 1935 and 1984 in Europe, the United States, and Japan. Scherer reviewed the results of these investigations and discovered that all studies that had investigated states that can be classified as 'elation' had generated remarkably consistent findings. That is, mean F0, F0 range, and F0 variability of speech in these emotional conditions increased without fail. With regards to the emotion type categorized as 'indifference', which is the exact opposite from 'elation,' he found decreases in mean F0 in studies which included this emotion state (although there had been few studies of this condition).

In a 1996 study, Banse and Scherer found further support for Scherer's 1986 observations. Mean F0 of the professional actors and actresses used in the 1996 study was located in the highest range for the 'intense' emotions such as 'elation.' It was positioned in the lowest range for 'contempt' and 'boredom.' Other emotions such as 'interest' were expressed in the middle range. Furthermore, when 12 advanced students from a professional acting school listened to the emotion portrayals by these actors for recognition accuracy, it was found that the accuracy rate of 'boredom' (76 percent), and 'interest' (75 percent) was among the highest. The acoustic demarcations of these emotions apparently were highly explicit and easy to recognize.

In Japan, in the 1970s, a few researchers such as Niwa (1970; 1971) and Utsuki (1976), examined how voice cues are correlated with types of emotion. These researches, however, appear to have been limited to studies carried out for the purpose of deciphering information derived from airplane pilots who were in emotional states, mainly funded by Japan Self-Defense Force. In the 1980s, researchers sporadically investigated speech containing emotions, and speech prosody of emotional expressions in Japanese. Investigators such as Ito (1986), Kitahara, Tohkura, *et al.* (1989) may have been inspired by research conducted in the West by emotion scholars such as Scherer.

However, it was not until the 1990s that a large amount of research commenced in Japan pertaining to the relationship between speech and emotion. By then, researchers in linguistics and speech sciences were showing great interest in how emotion influences human voice. They, too, exerted their efforts to develop a model to analyze both segmental and suprasegmental features of speech expressed with emotions. Such endeavors have been documented in numerous studies published in journals in the fields of ergonomics, electronics, information, and communication engineering as well as acoustics. More recently, one of the issues of the Phonetic Society of Japan's 2004 journal selected 'emotion and speech' as a special theme, featuring studies conducted from various standpoints of perception, audition, acoustics, and articulation of emotional speech. Contributors to the issue include D. Erickson, N. Campbell, and M. Teshigawara.

In both the United States and Japan, the most recent research on emotion expressed in speech has focused on investigating how accurately prosodic features expressing emotions can be incorporated into human speech recognition and speech synthesis. That machines are not emotional (while humans are) constrains their ability to communicate. This apparently is a key challenge for research in information sciences, where it has rapidly become one of the central research issues in recent years. Various groups of researchers in this field have addressed the subject from different viewpoints in their attempts to develop methods of detecting emotion and construct models that predict speech behavior in a range of emotional situations. Progress has been slow and often limited. However, these investigators continue to explore new ideas with the aim of improving such techniques and systems.

In the United States, Henton (the aforementioned speech researcher) joined the effort being made by researchers in information and communications sciences. Henton is currently a founder and chief technology officer of Talknowlogy, which delivers speech technology products, services, and consulting expertise. Henton has been frequently publishing her research on both recognition of synthesis of speech with emotion in *Speech Technology Magazine*. In Japan researchers (such as N. Campbell) affiliated with the Media Information Science Laboratories, at ATR (Advanced Telecommunications Research) have been conducting related investigations since the mid-1990s in Japan.

Cross-cultural Studies of Speech and Emotion

Additional cross-cultural studies involving Japanese, Europeans, and Americans have been conducted on various types of emotion. These studies predominantly show cross-linguistic accuracy in recognizing the types of emotion expressed.

In 1972, Beier and Zautra asked 52 American, 55 Polish, and 54 Japanese students to judge American speakers' vocal expressions in speech samples containing 48 expressions of six different emotions (happy, fear, sad, anger, indifference, and flirt) with four different lengths in utterances of 'hello,' 'good morning,' 'how are you,' and a sentence. These American, Polish, and Japanese students rated the tape-recorded speech which included 48 expressions with one repetition (the total of 96 expressions) in their home countries. The Polish and Japanese students who participated in this study were unfamiliar with the English language. Polish students agreed with Americans expressing these emotions 53 percent of the time, while Japanese students agreed with them 48 percent of the time. Beier and Zautra suggest that cultural information can be transmitted through the nonverbal vocal means of expression. These foreign informants clearly demonstrated agreement on the 'American' emotion items even though they were not as accurate as American informants.

Van Bezooijen, Otto, and Heenan (1983) examined cross-cultural recognizability of vocal portrayals of emotions produced by Dutch speakers. The results indicate that groups of approximately 40 young adult judges (from the Netherlands, Taiwan, and Japan) recognized the emotions portrayed with better than chance accuracy. The authors concluded that there are universally recognizable characteristics of vocal patterns of emotion. Even when confused about the portrayed emotions, the patterns of confusion that the judges demonstrated were similar across nations.

In 2001 Scherer, Banse, and Wallbott conducted a cross-cultural study of vocal emotion portrayals in nine different countries in Europe (Germany, Switzerland, Great Britain, the Netherlands, Italy, France, and Spain), the United States (California), and Asia (Indonesia). They had four professional German actors (two male, two female) articulate context free sentences expressing angry, sad, fearful, joyful, and neutral feelings. These artificially constructed sentences consisted of randomly arranged meaningless syllables from each of six European languages. They selected scenarios to elicit these emotions from the actors based on the particular type of situation, such as 'death of a loved one' for sadness. The total of 428 respondents in nine countries listened to a final stimulus set consisting of 30 sentences selected from 88 utterances after 29 students judged the naturalness of the stimulus at the University of Giessen, Germany. The number of informants in each country varied between 32 and 70. Their age ranged from 18 to 30 years; the male and female ratio was balanced.

The study found an overall accuracy of 66 percent across all emotions and countries, suggesting that similar inference rules for vocal expression exist across cultures. It was also found that the patterns of confusion were very similar across all countries. However, there was evidence that culture- and language-specific paralinguistic patterns may influence the process of decoding emotion types. The results show that recognition accuracy generally decreased as the linguistic differences from German increased.

Most recently, Sakuraba, Imaizumi, and Kakehi (2004) compared the acoustic features of voices used by 30 Japanese and American children (15 in each group) ranging in age between 4 and 10. They had these children utter the word '*pikachuu*', a popular Japanese animation character, while looking at differing images of this character portraying the emotions of happy, sad, angry as well as neutral. It is speculated that these researchers chose children as actors of targeted emotions with the assumption that they would be capable of unconsciously producing most natural utterances with appropriate emotions. The results show that the dynamic F0 range of these expressions of emotions in the two languages was similar even though the length of syllables varied. For example, the dynamic voice pitch ranges used to describe the emotion 'joy' in the image of '*pikachu*' were 229 Hz (330 Hz~547 Hz) for Japanese children and 252 Hz (289 Hz~541 Hz) for American children. By contrast, Japanese children utilized the dynamic voice pitch ranges of 179 Hz (179 Hz~358 Hz) and American children 81Hz (196 Hz~277Hz) to utter neutral emotion depicted by the image of '*pikachu*'. The elated emotion such as 'joy' was expressed with much wider voice pitch ranges than those used to express neutral emotion. Researchers claimed that the dynamic voice pitch range demonstrates common universal characteristics according to emotions types at least to a certain degree. The study also examined the recognition rate of these children's articulations of the same utterances by 28 adult Japanese and American English judges (14 in each set). Both sets of listeners recognized the emotions uttered by Japanese children with a better than chance accuracy.

To recapitulate the general tendency of the findings of all the aforementioned studies conducted on men's and women's voice pitch, it must be first noted that the researchers generally have found a consistent disparity in mean or median voice pitches between men and women across cultures when expressed in Hertz values. When these values found among American speakers are expressed in non-linear semitones, the gap diminishes drastically. Nonetheless, this change has been observed only in speech data largely derived from informants' vowel articulation and passage/constructed dialogue reading. Additionally, impromptu speech (which includes a scripted one) has been found to show overall lower pitch levels than the level found in oral reading of passages in all studies which included this speech type. This discrepancy was confirmed in Johns-Lewis's examination of pitch used by British English speakers in speech data consisting of three discourse types (of reading, acting, and conversing) documented in 1986. She found that conversational data demonstrated considerably lower mean pitch values with narrower pitch range than speech samples derived from reading or acting. In the following chapter, I present the importance of examining conversational speech data.

With regards to correlations between voice cues and emotion types, psychologists and linguists have found some consistency though they have faced continual challenges investigating this link. One such association is that between increase in mean F0, F0 range/ F0 variability of speech and the emotional conditions categorized as 'elation'. This particular correlation, which Scherer reviewed in 1986, has been evident in all studies. This connection was also highlighted in the 2004 cross-cultural study conducted on Japanese and American speakers. In addition, all of the multi-cultural perception studies reviewed here have found at least a better-than-chance accuracy in listeners' recognizing the types of emotion expressed. I shall return to the issue of correlations between voice pitch and emotion in Chapter 4.

Notes

1. A device that records oscillations, as of an electric current and voltage. *The American Heritage® Dictionary of the English Language*, Fourth Edition. Copyright © 2000 by Houghton Mifflin Company. Published by the Houghton Mifflin Company.
2. Creaky voice refers to 'a vocal effect produced by a very slow vibration of only one end of the vocal cords' (Crystal. D. (1997) *Dictionary of Linguistics and Phonetics*. Oxford. Blackwell Publishing, 98)
3. Chiba, T. (1934) *Research into the Nature and Scope of Accent in the Light of Experimental Phonetics*.
   Inoue, O. *The Journal of Phonetic Society of Japan*.
   Kobata, J. *The Journal of Mathematics and Physics*. VIII-1. IX-3.
4. Hideki Kasuya currently serves as the vice president of the Acoustical Society of Japan.
5. These values were not documented but obtained by personal communication with Kasuya.

6.   Examination involving inserting an instrument through the larynx.
7.   Weaver, by citing Scripture, notes that Scott was the first researcher who developed apparatus which recorded speech. According to Scripture, Scott's 1864 publication named his instrument 'phonautograph.' Readers who may be interested in a detailed description on the phonautograph will find it in Scripture's *The Elements of Experimental Phonetics on* pages 17 through 31.
8.   Weaver (1924: 49) states that it (the difference) has been much reduced by plotting the curves on the semi-logarithmic paper. In a semi-logarithmic graph, one axis has a logarithmic scale and the other axis has a linear scale. This means that Weaver plotted the measured fundamental frequency values logarithmically on the vertical axis and simply plotted 'male' and 'female' on the horizontal axis.
9.   The apparatus used in pitch analysis was a modification of that described by Metfessel, Simon, and Tiffin.

> Metfessel, M. (1927) Techniques for the objective study of vocal art. *Psychological Monograph* XXXVI: 1–40.

> Simon, C. T. (1927) The variability of consecutive wave lengths in vocal and instrumental sounds. *Psychological Monograph* XXXVI: 41–88.

> Lewis, D. and Tiffin, J. (1934) A psychophysical study of individual differences in speaking ability. *Archives of Speech* I: 13–60.

10. It is a passage designed for articulation exercise and it evidently includes all the normal sounds of spoken English. The full text of the 'Rainbow Passage' can be found in page 127 of the 2nd edition of Grant Fairbanks' *Voice and Articulation Drillbook*. New York: Harper & Row. The first paragraph reads as below:

> When the sunlight strikes raindrops in the air, they act as a prism
> and form a rainbow. The rainbow is a division of white light into
> many beautiful colors. These take the shape of a long round arch,
> with its path high above, and its two ends apparently beyond the
> horizon. There is , according to legend, a boiling pot of gold at
> one end. People look, but no one ever finds it. When a man
> looks for something beyond his reach, his friends say he is
> looking for the pot of gold at the end of the rainbow.

11. 'The FFI is an electronic device that samples the signal period of approximately every 33 ms and is equipped with a teletype unit that punches out the period data for transfer to IBM punch cards. The cards are computer processed and results in a read out of the geometric mean frequency and distribution standard deviation' (Saxman and Burke, 1967: 168).
12. Details of the phonellegraphic analysis method are described by Cowan (1936).
13. Richards' citation information is missing from page 5 in Olwen's publication.
14. See the section of 'Perception of voice pitch (linear and non-linear logarithmic scales)' in Chapter 3.

15. Pertaining to change in electrical resistance of skin resulting from mental processes which cause alterations in secretion of perspiration. ©From the *Hutchinson Encyclopaedia*, Helicon Publishing Ltd 2007.
16. Described on page 84 in Osgood, C. E., George J. S. and Percy, H. T. (1957) The semantic differential as a measurement instrument. In *The Measurement of Meaning*. Urbana, IL: University of Illinois Press.
17. A visual representation of a given set of sounds in the parameters of time, frequency and amplitude generated by the sound spectrograph. The sound spectrograph is an automatic sound wave analyzer and a basic research instrument widely used for the analysis and classification of human speech sounds.

3   Comparative Sociophonetic Research of Voice Pitch

Chapter 3 begins with an introduction of comparative examinations of Japanese and American voice pitch performed by previous researchers. These investigators are Hanley, Snidercor and Ringel (1966), Hanley and Snidercor (1967), Loveday (1981), Van Bezooijen (1995), and Yamazawa and Hollien (1992). They obtained their results from passages and constructed dialogues read by informants. Hanley, Snidercor and Ringel compared the median voice pitches of American, Japanese, Spanish, and Tagalog speakers. Loveday contrasted Japanese men's and women's voice pitch ranges with those of English men and women. Van Bezooijen conducted a perception test of Japanese and Dutch women's voice pitches by having both Japanese and Dutch listeners hear these women's voices. Additionally, Yamazawa and Hollien compared the speaking fundamental frequency means and distribution patterns of Japanese females with those of their Caucasian American counterparts.

Prior to discussing my studies of this volume, the definition of an intonation group (the prosodic unit which is utilized for pitch measurements) and the criteria used to identify an intonation group will be introduced. My main investigation consists of two parts: the preliminary study examining Japanese speakers and the final comparative study exploring both Japanese and American speakers. The chapter initially mentions the results of the 1998 pilot study (Yuasa, 1998). The chapter then presents the comparative study (Yuasa, 2001; 2002), which parsed conversational speech data elicited from both Japanese and American speakers. In both studies, two specific prosodic features were acoustically measured and analyzed. These were the width of pitch movements (how wide or narrow speakers' pitch movements expanded) as well as the levels of pitch (how high or low these movements reached) within an intonation group.

Studies Using Passages and Constructed Dialogues Read by Informants

Hanly was the first researcher who conducted a cross-linguistic study of voice characteristics. In 1951, he initially undertook an acoustic analysis of voice pitch characteristics from several regions in America where various dialects prevailed. Hanley then commenced an investigation in 1966 which had as its object the description of the same voice pitch attribute of male speakers of diverse languages (Spanish, Japanese, and American English) with Snidercore and Ringel. These researchers had eight male speakers of the foregoing languages read the 'Rainbow Passage' prepared in their own languages. They were students at the University of California, Los Angeles. The average age of the Japanese informants was 29 and that of Americans 20.5. Recordings were done in a sound treated room located at the University of California, Los Angeles. The result of this study indicates that the median pitch of Japanese male speakers (130.6 Hz) was *higher than* that of American males (105.6 Hz). The pitch variability of Japanese male speakers (2.8) in terms of semitone[1] was also found to be greater than that of their American counterparts.

Hanley proceeded with Snidercor in 1967 to examine female speakers of the previously described languages in order to compare the outcome with the result of the noted study. They selected four groups of informants (each of eight young women), from native speakers of Tagalog, Spanish, Japanese, and the standard American English. They were students at the University of California, Los Angeles, the University of California, Santa Barbara, and University of Southern California. They then recorded each informant performing a reading of the 'Rainbow Passage' aloud in her native tongue. Recordings were done in a sound treated room located at the University of California, Los Angeles. Median pitch level and standard deviation of distribution of measured F0 were collected on the Fundamental Frequency Indicator (FFI) installed at the University of Florida. The median pitch of American females was 203.6 Hz and that of Japanese females 225.2 Hz. The pitch variability in terms of pitch sigma semitone resulted in 2.7 for American females and 2.8 for Japanese females.

The results of these two studies by Hanley *et al.* demonstrated that there appear to be differences between Japanese and American men's and women's voice pitches. The outcome, however, is somewhat inconsistent with the previous findings of the investigations of these speakers' voice pitches. Japanese speakers' median pitch levels in Hanley *et al.*'s investigations are indeed similar to the average pitch levels obtained from informants in the 1968 study by Kasuya *et al.* The latter pitch levels, however, were derived from a vowel sound enunciated by the informants. Nevertheless, when the results by American informants were compared with outcomes rising from numerous acoustic analyses of American men's voice pitch performed prior to Henley *et al.*, their F0 measurements are considerably lower. Hanley *et al.*'s American male informants' median pitch (105.6 Hz) resembles the average median pitch of American males whose voices were regarded as masculine (100 Hz) in Terango's 1966 investigation. The median pitch of Hanley *et al.*'s American females (203.6 Hz) is similar to the average median frequency level (201 Hz) demonstrated by informants in the 1973 study by Linke, but is *much lower* than those found prior to Linke's investigation. Admittedly, the differences observed in Hanley *et al.*'s studies, nonetheless, do appear to be authentic ones. These differences ring true particularly in view of the fact that the speech data of these groups of informants who spoke Japanese and English were collected and analyzed within *the same* methodology framework.

In 1981, Loveday observed in his speech data, in which he acoustically measured F0, that his male Japanese informants used lower and flatter pitch movements compared to Englishmen's pitch movements. Only five Japanese (three males and two females) and five English informants were examined in this study. All the informants are college-educated. The British English speakers were considered as speakers of Received Pronunciation (traditionally viewed as the standard variety of British English). The Japanese informants were judged by Loveday to be capable of speaking a standard variety of their native language.

Loveday's informants' ages varied: Japanese females were 28 and 29; the British English females, 23 and 25; the Japanese males were 36, 42, and 44; and the British males were 24, 39, and 46. The informants played one of the two roles in a short prewritten dialogue which contained polite greetings ('Hello', 'Thank you very much', and 'Good-bye'). The average pitch movement width of three polite expressions examined on the sound spectrograph in terms of Hertz uttered by Loveday's three Japanese male informants was 15 Hz (highest mean: 100 Hz; lowest mean: 85.5 Hz). Conversely, the average pitch movement width of their English counterparts was 90.6 Hz (highest mean: 200 Hz; lowest mean: 109.4 Hz). Loveday's interpretation of the foregoing was that the Japanese men's presentation of an unemotional, self-restrained appearance was manifested in these low and flat pitch movements.

By contrast, Loveday's research findings revealed that Japanese women utilized an unnaturally high pitch as a mark of their 'daintiness'. Loveday maintains that in Japanese a high pitch serves to express a stereotypically female role. The mean pitch movement width of the same polite expressions which Loveday's two Japanese female informants produced was 96.7 Hz (highest mean: 376.7 Hz; lowest mean: 280 Hz). Their English counterparts generated an average pitch movement width of 86.7 Hz (highest mean: 250 Hz; lowest mean: 163.3 Hz).

I assume that the style of speech both the Japanese men and women utilized in this study was formal/negative politeness. The informants were asked to enact the role of someone who meets a non-intimate acquaintance on the street (who relocated to another neighborhood). Further, this register of the language used in this constructed dialogue was characterized by addressee honorifics (*desu*- and *masu*- sentence endings). Loveday's F0 measurement results, therefore, are regarded as an outcome acquired from speech emanating within a relatively formal context. They will be contrasted to part of the results of Yuasa's comparative study in the third section of this chapter.

Van Bezooijen's 1996 study (which focused on Japanese and Dutch women's pitches) revealed that Japanese listeners (both men and women) perceived Japanese women's medium and high pitch as more appealing than Dutch listeners (both men and women) did (260–63). Speakers were eight Dutch and eight Japanese women who were respectively either students or teachers at Dutch and Japanese universities. The average age of Japanese speakers was 33 and that of Dutch speakers 29. All speakers read the same 13-second-long narrative text consisting of a description of a house. The speech samples were modified so that the stimuli contained three different average pitch levels. The pitch manipulations were carried out using POSLA (Pitch Synchoronous Overlap and ADD) technique. The mean pitch of Dutch speakers was 185 Hz and that of Japanese counterparts 180 Hz.

In these speech samples, the average pitch levels were 155 Hz (low), 185 Hz (medium), and 218 Hz (high) for the Japanese women and 150 Hz (low), 180 Hz (medium), and 212 Hz (high) for the Dutch women. An equal number of Japanese and Dutch men and women listened to stimuli comprised of speech samples derived from these Japanese and Dutch speakers. They were 30 Dutch students at the University of Nijmegen (15 males and 15 females) and 30 Japanese students at the Dokkyo University.

The informants were asked to rate Japanese and Dutch speech samples on the scale of 'attractive'/'unattractive'. The outcome of Van Bezooijen's study will be re-introduced in later in this chapter to strengthen my interpretations for the female Japanese informants' voice pitch modulation patterns found in this volume's comparative study.

Yamazawa and Hollien (1992) compared information on the speaking fundamental frequency (SFF) means, variability, and distribution patterns of Japanese female and Caucasian speakers of American English. They investigated these features pertaining to voice pitch derived from standard passages read by 56 young women: 32 Japanese and 24 Americans (in either or both the Japanese and English languages). The average age of all the Japanese informants was 24.5 and that of Americans 23.5.

Japanese informants read a passage from *Donguri to Yamaneko* ('Wild cat and the Acorns') by Kenji Miyazawa while Americans read the 'Rainbow Passage'. The recordings were carried out either in a room with reasonably good acoustics characteristics located in Tokyo, Japan or in a sound treated room in the Institute for Advanced Study of the Communication Processes (IASPC), University of Florida, USA. The fundamental frequency of the recorded samples was obtained by means of the IASPC Fundamental Frequency Indicator (FFI-8) coupled to a PDP 11/23 computer.

One of their discoveries was that Japanese women exhibited a significantly higher mean speaking fundamental frequency than did their American counterparts. The other finding was that Japanese speakers utilized somewhat greater speaking fundamental frequency variability when speaking Japanese than their American counterparts did in speaking English. They concluded that the pitch accent aspect of Japanese resulted in the overall higher speaking fundamental frequency mean[2] and increased speaking fundamental frequency variability for these speakers.[3] Yamazawa and Hollien emphasized that such a difference in structural characteristics of the Japanese and English languages is a more tenable explanation than those related to other factors (such as physical size and psychological attribute) for the differences in SFF between female Japanese speakers and Caucasian speakers of American English.

Yamazawa and Hollien, however, did not examine these speaking fundamental frequency features exhibited by male Japanese speakers in order to verify their claim that the language specific factor is linked to higher speaking fundamental frequency means and greater speaking fundamental frequency variability. If speaking fundamental frequency means and variability were to be affected by the pitch accent aspect of the Japanese language, the aforementioned association must emerge regardless of the sex of Japanese speakers. Furthermore, an intonation group adopted as a F0 measurement unit for the present writer's studies (below) is defined so that those intrinsic accentual patterns of the Japanese languages will be included. Therefore, Yamazawa and Hollien's argument for a language-specific attribute will not be included in a discussion of the interpretation of voice pitch modulation patterns described in this volume's final comparative study.

Study Analyzing Speech Derived from Task-completion by Informants

In 1999, Ohara carried out a study of two types of speakers. The first were native speakers of Japanese who were competent speakers of American English. The second type consisted of native speakers of American English who were also competent in speaking Japanese. Each group consisting of ten subjects: five females and five males whose ages ranged from 26 to 42 for females and 26 to 36 for males. All of them were students at the University of Hawaii at Manoa. Ohara tape-recorded each subject when the subject was leaving a telephone message on an answering machine. The subjects were asked to leave messages in both Japanese and English for a professor and a friend. For all the messages, each subject called a set telephone number by using a telephone in the lab. The subjects were instructed to include the following information: (1) self identification; (2) explanation that they were looking for a book; (3) statement they could not find a book in the library; (4) requests to borrow the book; and (5) remark about calling back later. Ohara measured the fundamental frequency of each subject voice for each of the five segments of the message using the computer software, Signalyze, version 3.0.

All of the Japanese female subjects demonstrated higher mean fundamental frequency when speaking Japanese rather than in English, while talking to a professor as well as to a friend. The study also found that these female subjects, while speaking Japanese, exhibited higher fundamental frequency in the message to a professor than the message to a friend. By contrast, the fundamental frequency of the male Japanese subjects did not differ significantly across languages.

Similar tendencies were observed among English bilingual groups. Female English bilinguals employed a higher fundamental frequency in Japanese than in English. On the other hand, male English bilinguals demonstrated only minimal variation across languages and addressees.

Studies Utilizing Conversational Speech Data

The prosodic unit which is utilized for pitch measurements for my investigations, which utilized conversational speech data, is an 'intonation group'. I begin this section with the details of its definition, identification criteria for intonation group boundaries, phonetic criteria in determining intonation groups, and how a voice pitch movement of each intonation group was acoustically measured.

Intonation Group

There are terms comparable to the phrase 'intonation group' used for this study. They have been differently called in the literature – 'tone units' (Crystal, 1969), 'major/minor phrase's in Japanese (McCawley, 1968), 'tone groups' (Ladd, 1996), 'accentual phrases' (Pierrehumbert and Beckman, 1988), 'intonation units' (Du Bois *et al.*, 1993), and so forth. In addition, Cruttenden (1986) used the identical term 'intonation groups'. The notion 'intonation group' adopted for the studies of this book is similar to these terms although it is not exactly the same unit. While all of the above similar units (except for 'accentual phrases') are perceptual auditory units, the intonation group used here is an acoustically identified unit. For the purpose of this volume's studies, I define an intonation group as 'an acoustically measured prosodic unit occurring under a single unified intonation contour with only one primary F0 peak.' This means that the primary F0 peak can occur at any location of a single unified intonation contour: (1) in the beginning, (2) the middle, or (3) the end, as pictorially illustrated below:

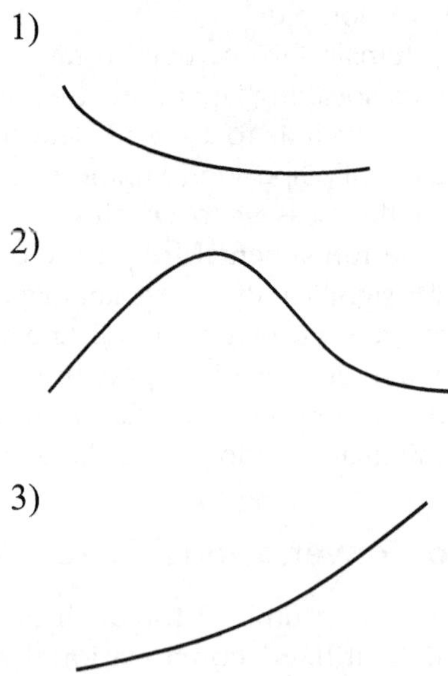

Cruttenden (1986: 36) describes criteria determining intonation-group boundaries as being two types: external and internal criteria. The external criteria are phonetic criteria (e.g., a pause) which application produces groups of utterances. The internal criteria represent internal structure which every intonation group possesses (e.g., a pitch movement to or from an accented syllable) and which accords with 'whole' intonation patterns.

For identification of intonation-group boundaries for the studies of this book, only external phonetic criteria set by Cruttenden is used. Cruttenden's external criteria are phonetic cues present at the boundaries: pauses, lengthening of the final syllables, and resetting of the baseline pitch level. However, intonation-group boundaries used for this study are not always determined according to his criteria. Since the main interest of this book's investigations is to examine the patterns of the pitch range fluctuations which speakers of Japanese employ, some of Cruttenden's concerns about determining the intonation-group boundaries in English are not relevant. The following subsections, showing how Cruttenden's standards are applied in determining intonation groups, will be demonstrated and examples obtained from the preliminary study will be provided.

Pauses

First of all, the forms of a pause can be divided into two categories: the unfilled pause (i.e. silence) and the filled pause. The latter involves the use of a central vowel (*schwa*) and a bilabial nasal [m], either alone or in combination of varying lengths in English. In Japanese, fillers, such as *anoo* ('well') and *eeto* ('let's see') commonly occur in filled pauses. Other fillers which occurred in my data in Japanese are *maa* ('well') and *dee* ('and').

Among the three types of pauses with which Cruttenden identifies, he considers only the first type as an intonation-group boundary indicator. He regards the latter two simple hesitation markers. However, for the purposes of my studies, all three types are considered as intonation-group markers. Cruttenden's three types of pauses with his examples as well as mine (selected from my Japanese speech data) are as follow (Boundaries are indicated by slash (/) ; periods (...) are hesitation markers) (Cruttenden. 1986: 37–42):

1. Pauses which occur at major constituent boundaries principally between clauses and between subject and predicate. Examples are:

> (1)   The Prince of Wales / is visiting Cardiff tomorrow. (Cruttenden, 1986: 38)

> (2)   *Senkoo wa / keezaigaku desita.* (Japanese Male 2) '(My) major was / economics.'

2. Pauses which occur before words of high lexical content or at point of low transitional probability. This kind of pause typically occurs before a minor constituent boundary within noun phrase, verb phrase, or adverbial phrase. For example:

> (3)   I saw a Bugatti in ... Cross Street yesterday. (Cruttenden, 1986: 38)

> (4)   *Ie no mawari ni / nanimo nain desu yo ne.* (Japanese Male 2) 'There is nothing / around (my) house, you know.'

3. Pauses which occur after the first word in an intonation group. This is a typical position for errors of performance, e.g., corrections of false starts and repetitions. It seems to serve a planning function, i.e., it is essentially a holding operation while the speaker plans the remainder of the sentence. Examples are as follows:

> (5)   I do like Elgar's violin concerto./ It's ... quite the most perfect work of its kind. (Cruttenden, 1986: 38)

> (6)   *Bizinesu maneezimento? Bizinesu maneezimento wa / nai desu kyoo wa.* (Japanese Male 2) 'Business Management? / Business Management, / there is no (Business Management class) today.'

Lengthening of the final syllables

Regardless of whether it is stressed or unstressed, the lengthened final syllable is often another phonetic cue to mark an intonation group. It may substitute for a filled pause and often carries a final pitch movement:

> (7)   On my way to the station (lengthening) / I met a man. (Cruttenden, 1986: 39)

> (8)   *Kozintekiniwa (lengthening) / toosi kankee o kiboo site imasu.* (Japanese Male 2) 'Personally, / I hope to do investment related (work).'

Resetting of the baseline pitch level

A change in pitch level and/or pitch direction among unaccented syllables generally indicates an intonation group boundary. Boundaries are marked when an utterance ended with high pitch and the beginning of a subsequent utterance is lower in pitch, or when an utterance ended with low pitch and the beginning of a subsequent utterance is higher in pitch (Cruttenden, 1986: 41). Examples are as shown below.

falling pitch + no pause + rising pitch

(9) John's not going tomorrow/but on Friday. (Cruttenden, 1986: 41)

falling pitch + no pause + rising pitch

(10) *Ruumumeeto no / amerika-zin no hito* ... (Japanese Female 4) '(My) roommate, an American ...'

For discussion of Japanese phrasal and intonational patterns, see the notions of minor and major phrases introduced by McCawley (1968), the abstraction of an accentual phrase postulated by Pierrehumbert and Beckman (1988), the intonation contours identified as signals of intonation unit boundaries by K. Matsumoto (1996: 81–2).

Voice Pitch Movement Measurement

After identifying intonation group boundaries based on the external criteria (phonetic cues present at the boundaries as described in the previous section), only the voiced components were ascertained for analyses by observing spectrographic images of intonation groups. After the CSL (Computerized Speech Lab) extracted F0s distributed in an intonation group, the highest (topline) and lowest (baseline) F0s were recorded. The entire procedure was performed in the Phonology Laboratory at the University of California, Berkeley. An example of this measurement procedure is shown in Figure 3.1. In this example, a female Japanese informant uttered *Nani kore?* (What's this?) with highest F0 of 319Hz and lowest F0 of 216Hz:

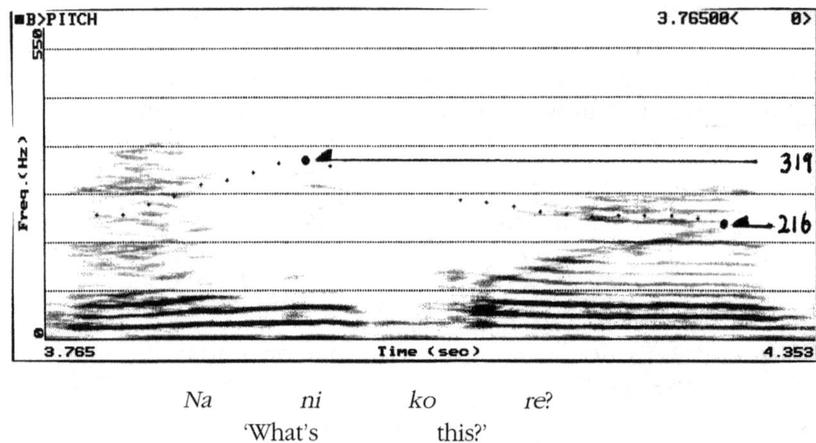

Na   ni   ko   re?
'What's   this?'

Figure 3.1 A sample of a spectrographic analysis with pitch extraction of an utterance, 'What's this?' in Japanese made by a Japanese informant.

The Preliminary Study

In the preliminary study (Yuasa, 1998) I examined Japanese speakers' pitch movements as employed in two types of conversations (with familiar and unfamiliar interlocutors). The informants' familiar interlocutors were their colleagues. Speech data were obtained from eight (four males and females) relatively young employees of major Japanese corporations temporarily residing in Hawaii, USA. The male unfamiliar interlocutor was the vice president of the Japan-America Institute of Management Sciences located in Hawaii. The female unfamiliar interlocutor was an instructor teaching at the same institute. The topics[4] of these two types of speech are at least similar to each other, if not identical, since all the topics are concerned with daily life.

I found that a narrower pitch movement was used more frequently between interlocutors. This outcome was consistent *regardless of the sex of the interlocutors.* By contrast, a wider pitch movement was used more frequently between familiar interlocutors. The informants conversed with interlocutors of the same sex.

For example, see the following extracts in which the male informant (M1) discusses the same topic (his desire to ride a large motorcycle) with unfamiliar and familiar interlocutors respectively. In the first extract, M1 maintains narrower pitch ranges in expressing his desire to the vice president (VP) of his school:

(11) (a) VP: *Kotira, Haaree Dabiddoson toka?*
'How about Harley Davidson?'

(b) M1: *Soo desu ne. Dekireba, Haaree ni **notte mitai ndesu***.
      15.6Hz   26Hz   25.6Hz   34Hz
'That's right. If possible, **I would like to ride** Harley.'

Compare this to the subsequent extract where M1 maintains considerably wider pitch ranges with a fellow informant (M2), again in communicating his wish:

(12) (a) M2: *Ii no atta?*
'Did you find a good one (motorcycle)?'

(b) M1: ***Hosii yatu** wa ookii yatu nan da kedo, supootusutaa sika*.

     129.5Hz   89Hz   67Hz
'The one I want is a big one, but only Sportstar (is the cheap one).'

Figures 3.2 and 3.3 display the foregoing. They demonstrate the differences in distribution of occurrences of pitch movements counted in intervals of 25 Hz between conversations held with an unfamiliar interlocutor (male) and familiar interlocutors according to the informants' gender.

The comparative study

Acoustically analyzing spontaneous speech such as conversational speech data (as opposed to passages and dialogues read by informants) requires additional caution. I took extra care in reviewing some basic

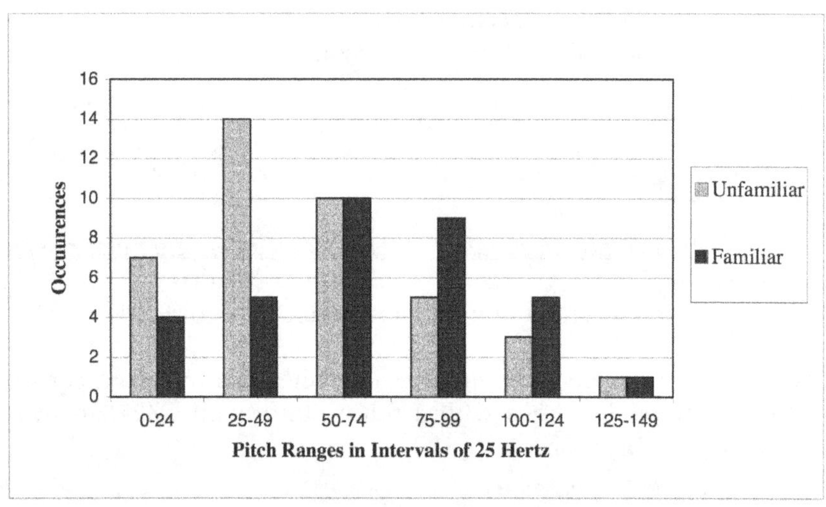

Figure 3.2 Japanese males' pitch movements in Hz.

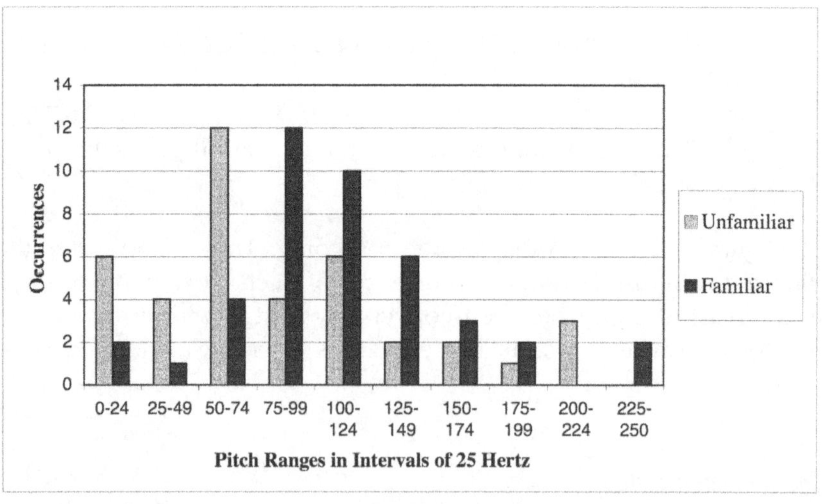

Figure 3.3 Japanese females' pitch movements in Hz.

concepts and information which were both necessary for and relevant to the acoustic phonetic analysis of such speech data. Before I proceed to presenting my comparative investigation, the following issues with regard to acoustically measuring voice pitch will be discussed: 1) intrinsic pitch differences; 2) just noticeable differences (JND) of pitch; 3) segmental factors affecting pitch measurements; 4) pitch range (register); and 5) perception of pitch (Linear and Non-Linear Logarithmic Scales).

Technical Issues on Acoustic Analyses of Conversational Speech Data

Intrinsic pitch (F0) differences in sentences and connected speech Intrinsic pitch or F0 difference refers to the observation that high vowels (such as [u] or [i]) tend to have a slightly higher F0 than low vowels (such as [a]) in the same phonetic context. Among the F0 measurements obtained from the data collected for the present study there are occasions of very narrow F0 range of less than 10 Hz produced by male informants and less than 30 Hz or 20 Hz by female informants. They typically occur at the end of complete utterances. The criteria which will be used to determine whether or not these very narrow F0s are results of intrinsic F0 effect are presented in the following sections.

The studies have shown that the effect of Intrinsic F0 is relatively small. While the range of F0 (pitch register) used by an individual in normal speech typically has been demonstrated to range from one-half to one-and-one-half octaves, the intrinsic F0 differences between vowels are one or two semitones (twelve semitones equal one octave). There have been numerous studies which document the existence of the intrinsic F0 effect in various European, African, and Asian languages (English by Ohala, 1973; Taiwanese Chinese by Zee, 1978; Yoruba by Hombert, 1977).

All of these studies used either isolated words or words in a set carrier phrase (e.g., 'Say the word peep again' as in Lehiste and Peterson (1961) for their investigations (Shadle, 1985). For example, an average female F0 range for normal speech is from 150 Hz to 300 Hz (Catford, 1977). Typical F0 differences between [u] and [a] are between 10 Hz and 30 Hz (one to two semitones) reported by Petersen (1976) in the Danish language.

With the use of fluent readings (English) by two speakers of 20-minute essays Umeda's 1981 study reported that there were no consistent intrinsic F0 effects. In her study she controlled for segmental (consonantal) context, but did not control for intentional effects, such as lexical stress, sentence stress, or declination. Ladd and Silverman (1984) pointed out that the changes in F0 due to declination are likely to eliminate the typical intrinsic F0 effect of her study.

Ladd and Silverman then compared readings of three paragraphs with words in a carrier sentence by four German informants. They found that the intrinsic F0 differences are smaller in the connected speech condition than in the carrier sentence condition. They controlled for phrase position and stress in the connected speech by locating test pairs in different prosodic environments. They concluded that low pitch rather than low-stress or phrase-final position is the relevant factor.

Shadle (1985) controlled for the semantic, consonantal, and prosodic environment for the sentences (English) which she used for her study. She observed that the intrinsic F0 difference decreased significantly in an unaccented final position in readings of these sentences by four informants. She suggests that both the lack of accent and the lower F0 caused the reduction in the intrinsic F0 difference.

The speech data used for the main study of this book is spontaneously produced speech, which can be regarded as a type of connected speech with a combination of fluency and hesitancy. Data is not controlled for any of the environmental factors which the investigators of the intrinsic F0 effects have manipulated. Thus, it is almost impossible to claim whether or not those exceptionally narrow F0 differences are merely differences between the intrinsic F0 of high and low vowels. Furthermore, those extremely narrow F0 ranges in the present study's data typically occurred at the end of complete sentences or utterances. Even if they are the suspected cases of intrinsic F0 differences, the measurement would not be likely to demonstrate the typical intrinsic F0 differences (mainly due to the effect of declination, as it appears to be the case of Umeda's study). The criteria which determine whether or not very narrow F0s are intrinsic F0 differences for the volume's main investigation are as follows.

In Petersen's study typical F0 differences between [u] and [a] in isolated words are between 10 Hz and 30 Hz (1–2 semitones)[5] in the Danish language. If an F0 range measured is narrower than 10 Hz for male speakers (or 30 Hz for female speakers), whether or not the vowel of the highest F0 is a high vowel ([i] or [u]) and the vowel of the lowest F0s is a low vowel ([a]) will be examined. If it is the case, whether or not the F0 range is located in the final phrase of an utterance will be inspected. If so, the F0 range may have been simply suppressed due to declination (Umeda, 1981; Shadle, 1985). Alternatively whether or not the F0 range occurred at a relatively lower pitch level for the particular speaker will also be examined. If it did, then low pitch effect (Ladd and Silverman, 1984) would the likely cause of the narrow F0 range. Only if none of the above conditions apply, then the possibility of intrinsic F0 difference will be considered.

Just noticeable difference in F0 The results of Klatt's study (1972) in JND (just-noticeable difference) in F0 indicate that the subjects can detect a change of 2.0 Hz when the F0 contour is a linear descending ramp (32 Hz/sec). Klatt used a number of 250-msec segments of the synthetic vowel /e/ differing only in F0. The results further demonstrate that sensitivity to rate of change of F0 in linear ramps was excellent (1.5 Hz) when one ramp increased and the other decreased (12 Hz/sec), creating a flat slope.

Although JND in natural speech is expected to be larger than the outcome of Klatt's study of synthetically-generated speech segments, no information could be obtained since there has not been any investigation to date into the phenomenon of JND in connected speech.

None of the notably narrow pitch ranges which have been measured for this volume's comparative study are narrower than 5 Hz for male speakers and 15 Hz for female speakers. It will be assumed that listeners are able to perceive these very narrow F0 ranges as narrow pitch modulations – not as completely flat pitch.

Segmental factors affecting F0 measurements One of the characteristics of fundamental frequency is that whether or not adjacent consonants are voiced affects the fundamental frequency of voiced sounds (Cruttenden, 1986: 4). Vowels, particularly, have a higher fundamental frequency when preceded by voiceless consonants than when preceded by a voiced consonant (Lehiste and Peterson, 1961). Lehiste and Peterson further found that the fundamental frequency peak is located at the beginning of the vowel following voiceless consonants and not in the middle of the vowel as after voiced consonants. Cruttenden, however, points out that the effects of characteristics such as this are lessened when a listener is listening to the meaning of an overall pitch pattern. For the purpose of the comparative study of this book, the first F0 measurements immediately following voiceless consonants will not be recorded. Instead, the second F0 measurements will be used for pitch movement calculations.

F0 range (voice pitch register) Jassem (1971) investigated what he calls the 'compass' of the speaking voice. He utilized a text of about 50 seconds long spoken naturally and unemotionally twice by ten males. Compass is defined by him as 'the width of F0 range'. Based on the short-term average F0 values[6] obtained, he demonstrated the useful property of the standard deviation (SD) in statistical calculation of the compass of the speaking voice.

He observed in his samples that a range of the values of the variable within two standard deviations of the mean represents approximately 95 percent of all observations. The values of the variable left outside the range between the mean +2 SD and the mean –2 SD are the least frequent ones. They are so rare that the occurrence of any of them is largely a matter of chance. He concludes that the values of F0 of twice the standard deviation above and twice the standard deviation below the mean should measure its compass.

This method of calculating F0 range has been adopted by a number of researchers such as Gilbert and Weismer (1974), de Pinto and Hollien (1982), and Henton (1989) for their studies of female speakers' F0 range.

Patterson (1999) and Ladd *et al.* (1985) refuted Jassem's idea. They argued that the mean and standard deviation do not adequately capture important differences in the pitch range of different speakers (Ladd *et al.*, 1985). They also claimed that such measures do not account for the fact that F0 values often have a non-normal distribution.

In Patterson's study, listeners are presented with recorded neutral and unemotional passages. They were asked to judge how much adjectives (e.g., confident, harsh, expressive, happy, etc.) characterized the voice on a seven point scale. He then correlated judgments of speaker characteristics with a variety of measurable pitch range parameters. These parameters coincide with two partially independent dimensions of variation called 'level' and 'span' which are used to describe pitch range (Ladd, 1996). F0 values were extracted at hand-marked locations corresponding to sentence initial peaks (High), other accent peaks (Mid), valleys (Low) and sentence final lows (Fall) in an idealized speaker contour. For F0 level, L and F which were considered as the sufficient bottom of the range, were measured. For F0 span, H–F, H–L, M–F, and M–L were measured.

Patterson found that the sentence final low was the slightly better measure of level. The best measure of span was the difference between average non-initial accent peak and average post-accent valley (M–L). He concluded that two linguistically motivated, partially independent dimensions of variation (level and span) better characterize the communicative effect of pitch range (compared with the single dimension of just highest–lowest F0). Clark (1999) further supported the idealized speaker contour with impressionistically landmarked locations of (H), (M), (L), and (F). He had found in his study of a newscaster's speech that phrase initial and final tone groups differ significantly from tone groups which are phrase medial.

However, in natural conversations this idealized contour is seldom realized. First, intonation groups are often fragmented by pauses and lengthening of final syllables. Second, intonation groups which represent sequences of phrases and clauses sometimes include a contextual or emotional emphasis which turns the final low into high, making realization of this idealized contour impossible.

Furthermore, Patterson compared the correlation between F0 span measures based on M–L difference and listener judgments with the correlation between measures of F0 span using other standards (90 percent range, 80 percent range, and four standard deviations) and listener ratings. Contrary to his observations, the correlation between the measures and listener assessments based on four standard deviations was *almost* as strong as correlation using M–L distance compared with those which employed the other basis. In other words, in terms of strength of the correlation there seems to be an obvious rift between M–L range and four standard deviations *versus* the 90 percent range and the 80 percent range.

Spontaneously occurring speech data such as the one that is considered for the comparative study of this volume tends to occasionally contain a very large Standard Deviation. This causes the 3.5 SDs or 4 SDs calculation to sporadically exceed the speaker's whole pitch range. Utilizing the mean and the Standard Deviation does not appear to be the appropriate vehicle to present my data. According to Graddol and Swann, 'listeners are extremely sensitive to the average pitch of a speaker's voice' (Graddol and Swann, 1989: 19). However, Graddol also mentioned that a pitch distribution tends to be positively skewed, containing more occurrences at lower than higher fundamental frequencies (1986: 225). Graddol and Swann (1983: 356–7) reported the median measure in preference to the mean since they consider it a more appropriate procedure to present distributions that are skewed. Thus, I chose to examine median values which are very similar to mean values. I focused on the median values which fall into the 50th percentile of all the pitch movements measured. If the median values of range measures for each speaker did not fall into the 50th percentile, values which fall closest to the 50th percentile (such as 52nd and 48th) were selected.

Perception of Voice Pitch (Linear and Non-linear Logarithmic Scales)

The human ear has been claimed to respond to speech sounds logarithmically rather than linearly (e.g., Graddol, 1986). In intonation research, pitch of speech has either been expressed on a linear scale (Hz) or on a logarithmic semitonal scale (Hermes and van Gestel, 1991). Rietveld and Gussenhoven in 1985 found that when judging prominence their informants tended to agree with each other more on a Hertz scale than with a scale of semitones. Graddol (1986: 228) believes that a logarithmic scale (as opposed to linear scale) is more preferable when measuring up intervals in pitch at different pitch registers, particularly, of male and female speakers. Expressing pitch logarithmically means is to say that intervals in pitch produced at a higher pitch register are perceived narrower than those generated at a lower pitch register by human ears. In other words, the pitch interval between two notes depends on the ratio of the two frequencies (e.g., from 100 Hz to 200 Hz (a ratio of 1 : 2) and 200 Hz, and 400 Hz are equal intervals of pitch). In the following section, types of non-linear scales, regardless of whether they are fully logarithmic or not, which have been used in hearing and intonation research are briefly introduced.

In intonation research, pitch of speech has been expressed primarily in three frequency scales. These scales are linear (Hz), logarithmic (semitones), and the ERB (Equivalent Rectangular Bandwidth) rate (a scale that is in between linear and logarithmic) scales.

Acoustical scale Since pitch is a subjective attribute of a stimulus, it cannot be measured directly (Moore 1997: 3). Acoustic phonetics (the study of physical properties of speech sound) makes pitch measurement possible through instrumental techniques. When variations in air pressure (which sounds consists of) reach the ear and cause the eardrum to vibrate, they form sound waves. The pitch of a sound depends on the rate of vibration of the vocal cords. Each opening and closing of the vocal cords causes a peak of air pressure in the sound wave. Thus, the pitch is closely related to the repetition rate (frequency) of this sound waveform. That is, the higher the frequency, the higher the pitch. The frequency is the number of times per second the waveform repeats itself. For speech sounds (periodic complex tones) this corresponds to the fundamental frequency (F0). The pitch of a speaker's voice coincides with fundamental frequency and is expressed as units of Hertz on a linear scale.

Musical scale Pitch is defined as 'that attribute of auditory sensation in terms of which sounds may be ordered on a musical scale from low to high' (Crystal, 1997: 294). Variations in pitch generate a sense of melody. Thus, in music perception, the relative distance between two tones is expressed in a musical interval such as semitones and the octave. An octave equals 12 semitones and a semitone corresponds to a frequency ratio of 1.059 (Rossing, 1982: 153–65). This musical scale uses a non-linear logarithmic frequency scale. An equation which converts Hertz into semitones is:

Semitones = 39.89 × log (F0/F0 ref.)

where F0 is the highest value in the range in Hz, and F0 ref. is the lowest value of the range, in Hz.

Psychoacoustic scale In psychoacoustics (the study that combines the study of the physical properties of speech sound and the study of human auditory system), the scale that is derived from measurements of the frequency selectivity of the human auditory system has been used. The newest variety of the scale is the Equivalent Rectangular Bandwidth (ERB) rate scale (Patterson, 1976; Moore and Glasberg, 1983; Glasberg and Moore, 1990). For the frequencies below 500Hz, the ERB-rate scale is neither linear nor non-linear logarithmic, but something in between (Hermes and van Gestel, 1991). An equation describing the values of the ERB as a function of frequency (Glasberg and Moore, 1990: 114) is:

E (number of ERBs) = 21.4log10 (4.37F + 1)
where F is frequency in kHz.

As female and male voices differ by almost one octave, the difference between these scales can create considerable discrepancies (Glasberg and Moore, 1990: 98). For example in a male voice, if a linear scale were used, pitch between note with frequencies 120 Hz and 180 Hz would correspond to the difference in pitch with note with frequencies of 240 Hz and 300 Hz in a female voice. If a logarithmic scale were used, a span from 240 Hz to 360 Hz would represent the same distance. On the ERB-rate scale, a distance from 240 Hz to 325 Hz would be required to produce the equal result. Figure 3.4 illustrates these differences between the three pitch scales:

There have been several studies conducted by researchers in sociophonetics and psychoacoustics which have claimed that the human ear evaluates pitch range on a non-linear logarithmic, rather than

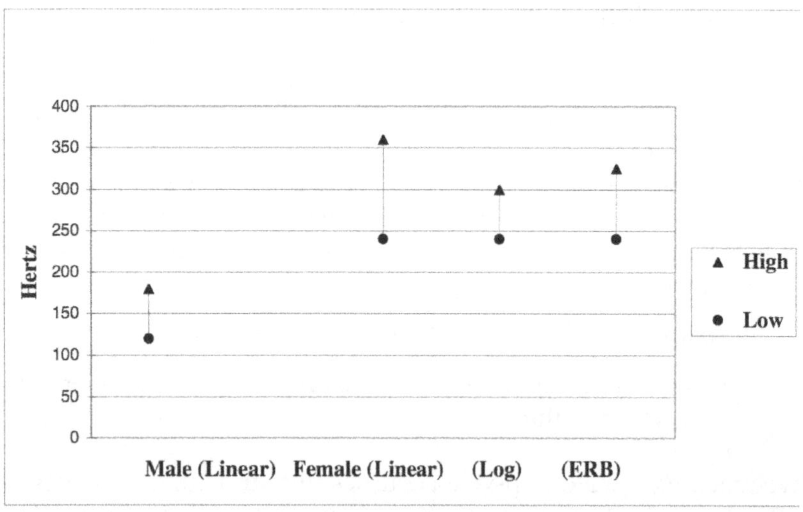

Figure 3.4 Female pitch ranges contrasted in linear, logarithmic, and ERB-rate scales in terms of Hz (linear) relative to male pitch range

linear scale. Rietveld and Gossenhoven (1985) set up an experiment to determine whether 'prominence-lending' pitch movements should be expressed in Hz or in semitones. They concluded that prominence judgments of their informants were in better agreement with a Hz scale than with a scale of semitones. This result was based on comparisons of the prominence of syllables with pitch movements in different frequency regions. However, their stimulus set comprised only sentences recorded from a female speaker which were resynthesized in an equal or in a lower pitch register. They noted that it would be premature to conclude that prominence-lending pitch movements should be expressed in Hertz. Choosing between the linear (Hz) and log (semitones) scales, Graddol (1986: 228) concluded that, 'whenever intervals in pitch must be compared at different frequencies, a log scale is to be preferred.' He averred that the extent of pitch range used by most women in his study seems to be rather small compared to that used by most men. This is smaller when expressed in semitones, but larger when expressed in linear scale (ibid.).

In order to decide on which scale the excursions of pitch movement are perceived, Hermes and van Gestel (1991) had their informants adjust the variable excursion size of a pitch movement. The informants compared the stimulus to the fixed excursion size of a pitch movement in a test stimulus resynthesized in a different frequency register. This was done both in sessions in which the test stimulus was in low register (while the comparison stimulus was in a high register) and for sessions in which the test stimulus was in a high register (while the comparison stimulus was in a low register). The results show that pitch movements in speech intonation can best be expressed in the ERB-rate scale, a scale that is derived from the frequency selectivity of the auditory system.

The frequency scales developed from the frequency selectivity of the auditory system are correlated with distances along the basilar membrane (Greenwood, 1961; 1990), one of the membranes which divide the cochlea located in the inner ear. The ERB-rate scale appears to be thus far the most appropriate for predicting equal perceptual prominence made by pitch movements in different (male and female) registers (Nooteboom, 1997: 645). The ERB-rate scales will be used to convert F0 measurements in Hertz for the analyses of the volume's comparative study. The converted E values of the ERB-rate scale will be adopted in performing cross-gender comparisons. However, this study seeks to compare the results of the analyses of the same sex voice pitch in terms of Hertz values on the linear scale.

Methodology

Data base The final comparative study conducted in this volume explores voice pitch ranges of men and women across languages (American English and Japanese). The first collection of speech data consists of two sets of conversations by Japanese male and female speakers: conversations between interlocutors who know each other and those who do not know. The second set of data was collected from conversations held between familiar speakers of American English.

Informants Nine relatively young American and Japanese males and females who are speakers of the standard variation of their languages held conversations. American informants are individuals in their 20s and 30s. They include graduate students at the University of California, Berkeley as well as non-student informants. The average age of American informants was 29. Japanese informants were primarily interns in their 20s and 30s recruited from the Japan Pacific Resource Networks in Oakland. They also included both undergraduate and graduate students at the University of California, Berkeley. All Japanese informants were considered socio-culturally Japanese based on their consistent usage of honorifics and formal mannerisms during interactions with unfamiliar interlocutors. Two speakers who did not meet these criteria were eliminated.

Other than age, homogeneity of the informants was controlled by the fact that they are speakers of standard American English or Japanese. American English, which the informants spoke, was mostly a Californian variety. Some informants were speakers of more than one variety of a language (e.g., regional or vernacular). Those who did not meet this criterion were eliminated from the study. American males and females conversed with familiar interlocutors. In the case of Japanese informants, they conversed with both familiar and unfamiliar interlocutors of mixed sex. The unfamiliar interlocutors were not only unfamiliar with the informants but also older and had higher statuses than the informants. They are either visiting scholars from Japanese universities or older Japanese individuals who are in various professions in San Francisco Bay Area. The average age of Japanese informants was 27.5. The sex of the interlocutors was mixed for both American and Japanese groups.[7]

Procedure The length of the conversations was approximately ten minutes. The conversations took place in a comfortable lounge or living room rather than in a recording booth in order to make the informants feel that they were engaging in natural conversations, not artificial ones. To achieve recordings of high enough quality for acoustic analysis, a miniature microphone was attached to the area of the informants' throats where the vocal cords are located with a loop around their necks. The topic the conversations was controlled: the informants talked only about food: an emotionally non-provocative but not uninteresting topic.

Voice pitch range measurement Forty to fifty consecutive intonation groups (approximately one minute long) were randomly selected from each conversation for pitch range analysis. This length was chosen because several studies conducted on F0 statistics of long-term parameters surveyed by Nolan (1983: 123) suggest that a minimum length of 40 seconds is necessary in order to obtain a veritable portrayal of speaker characteristics. In an individual case, according to Nolan, there may be some F0 variations between speech samples up to a period of 60 seconds. However, they diminish in the face of increasing sample length. In a sample length of longer than 60 seconds, very little variation is expected.

In measuring the highest and lowest points of pitch I followed the standards I had set above for such acoustics phonetics issues as intrinsic pitch differences, just noticeable pitch differences (JND) and segmental factor affecting pitch measurements. As noted earlier, median values of range measures for each informant, the value that fell into the 50th percentile or the values closest to this percentile, were used for statistics.

Conversion of measurements from linear into non-linear scales The acoustically measured F0 values in terms of Hz (a linear scale) were converted into only E values in the ERB-rate scale. As mentioned earlier, this is the scale which is considered in the field of psychoacoustics as the most appropriate scale for human speech perception for the purpose of comparing two differing male and female pitch registers. This final comparative investigation of this books focuses on median values in the linear Hertz and the ERB-rate scale.

Results

Japanese informants For Japanese speakers, the result of the preliminary study was identical to the outcome of the volume's comparative study. It was again found that when the Japanese spoke with *familiar* interlocutors, both men and women's pitch movements widened. Japanese males' average median pitch movement of 1.27 (in terms of E values) expanded to 1.81 when they conversed with familiar interlocutors. Similarly, the average median pitch movement of Japanese females was 1.52; during conversations with familiar interlocutors it was expressed as 2.23. Figure 3.5 displays differences in average median pitch movements expressed in the ERB-rate scale used by male and female Japanese informants in conversing with familiar and unfamiliar interlocutors. Moreover, female Japanese informants adopted narrow pitch movements at much higher frequencies than male Japanese informants during conversations with unfamiliar interlocutors. Figure 3.10 demonstrates the locations of median pitch movements of male and female Japanese informants.

Cross-cultural comparison The following result was obtained on measurements derived from conversations held between *familiar* interlocutors by informants *across languages*:

> In terms of all the values of the ERB, the pitch movements used by the Japanese speakers are generally wider than those of Americans. Figures 3.6 and 3.7 display average median pitch movements presented in both Hz and E values of the ERB-rate for Japanese and American informants across gender.

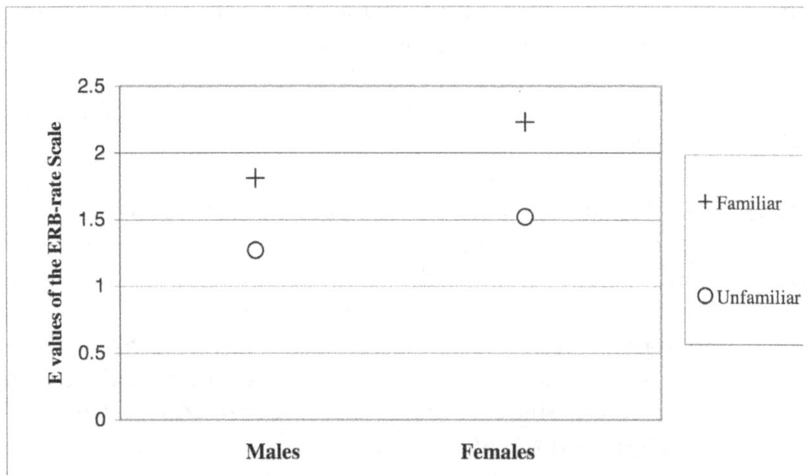

Figure 3.5 Average median pitch movements used by Japanese informants with familiar and unfamiliar interlocutors.

Interestingly, when the average lowest pitch levels for males and the average highest pitch levels for females are compared, the following outcome resulted:

> In terms of Hertz values of the linear scale, Japanese males' average lowest pitch level was 91.81 Hz, which was lower than that of American males (101.24 Hz). Moreover, Japanese males' average lowest pitch level was 89.45 Hz when conversing with *unfamiliar* interlocutors, which was even lower than the level evidenced during conversations with *familiar* interlocutors. However, the difference between the average lowest and highest pitch levels for Japanese males (91.81 Hz ~ 161.96 Hz) was wider than that of their American counterparts' (101.23 Hz ~ 149.37 Hz).
>
> By contrast, Japanese females' average highest pitch level (184.85 Hz) was higher than that of their American counterparts (172.29 Hz). A similar result was also obtained when they conversed with *unfamiliar* interlocutors. Their average highest pitch level was 180.79 Hz. Furthermore, the difference between the average lowest and highest pitch levels of Japanese females (184.85 Hz ~ 305.45 Hz) was correspondingly wider than that of American female's (172.29 Hz ~ 250.24 Hz).

Figures 3.6 and 3.7 illustrate these outcomes.

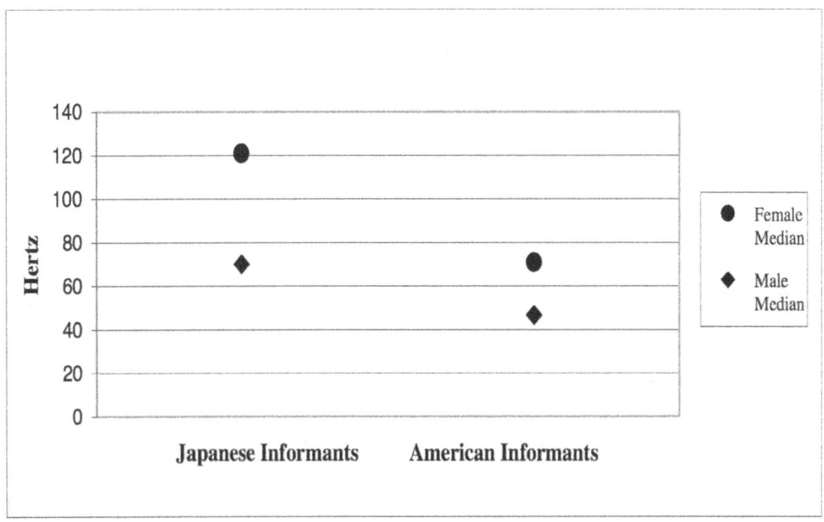

Figure 3.6 Average median pitch movements of Japanese and American informants in Hz

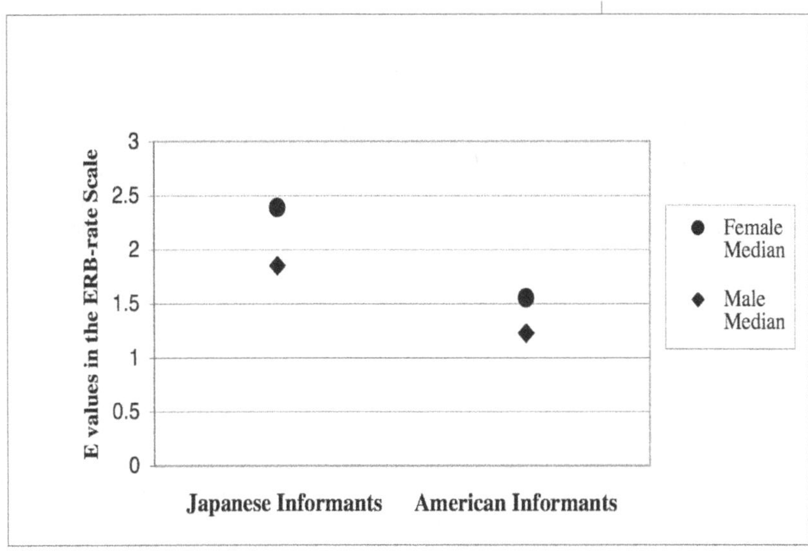

Figure 3.7 Average median pitch movements Japanese and American informants in ERB-rate scale

Gender-based comparison Result based on measurements gathered from conversations held between *familiar* interlocutors by informants *across gender* is:

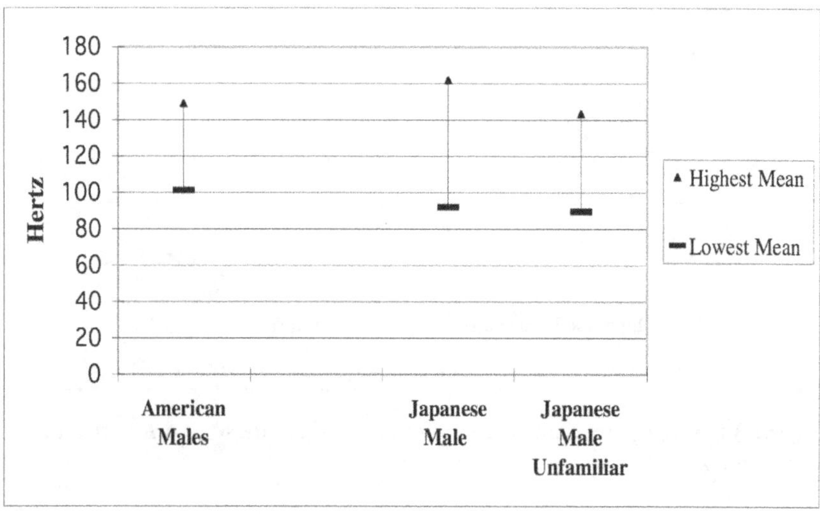

Figure 3.8 Average lowest voice pitch levels of Japanese and American male informants

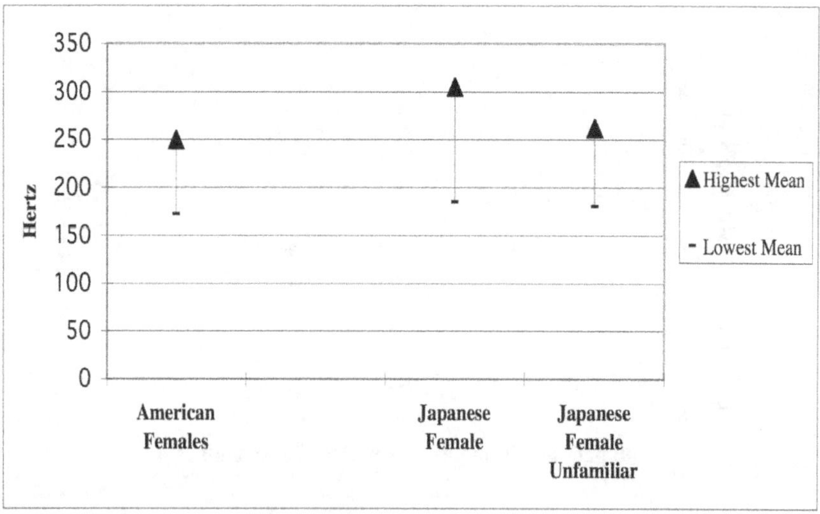

Figure 3.9 Average highest voice pitch levels of Japanese and American male informants

> When measurements in Hertz were converted into the ERB-rate
> values, the pitch ranges which females utilized are slightly wider
> than and those which males adopted in each language. However,
> the difference was not as large (particularly between Japanese
> male and females) compared with that in Hertz value.

Figures 3.8 and 3.9 also demonstrate the foregoing.

Maximum pitch movements and highest pitch levels A maximum pitch movement (the size of the maximum excursion) which each speaker utilized was also examined. The reason that the maximum pitch movement is at stake here stems from the fact that a pitch distribution is likely to be positively skewed (Graddol, 1986: 225). As mentioned earlier, this means that speaks tend to use pitch movements at the lower end of their whole range. Thus, large pitch movements that require reaching high pitch levels are expected to occur only occasionally. The standard practice in pitch range research dictates that the elimination of extreme pitch values. Since listeners are sensitive to the average pitch of a speaker's voice (Graddol 1986: 19), it is reasoned that including occasional extreme measurements may make the results a less accurate representation of listeners' subjective impressions of pitch. However, investigating these infrequent pitch movements with extreme pitch values is useful in elucidating the emphatic intonation which people may perceive from women's voice pitch patterns.

The maximum pitch movement, which contains the largest pitch expansion value of all the range measurements for each informant, was extracted. The maximum pitch movement was then compared with the movement that was used in the median pitch range. In terms of the values in the ERB-scale, the maximum pitch movements adopted by American women tend to be much larger than those used by American men. They are nearly twice as wide as those of their male counterparts. By contrast, large pitch movements similar to those utilized by American women were observed in both Japanese men and women. The average maximum pitch movement of Japanese men was, in fact, slightly larger than that of Japanese women. Figure 3.10 demonstrates the contrast between pitch movements used by all four groups (female American, male American, female Japanese, and male Japanese) in terms of average median pitch movements and maximum pitch movements used by the same informants.

The maximum pitch ranges adopted by American women tend to be much larger than those used by American men. They are nearly twice as wide as those of their male counterparts. By contrast, large pitch move-

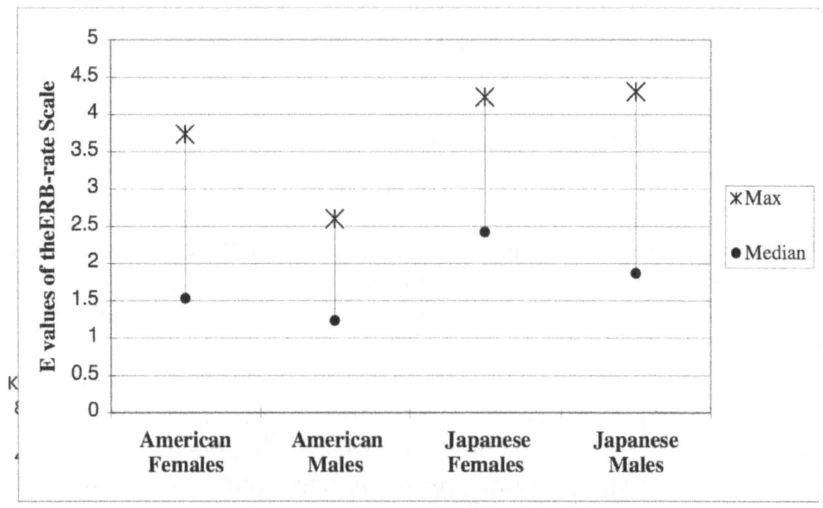

Figure 3.10 Maximum pitch range values as compared with median values obtained from Japanese and American informants

ments similar to those utilized by American women were observed in both Japanese men and women. The average maximum pitch movement of Japanese men was, in fact, slightly larger than that of Japanese women. Subsequently, attention was tuned to Japanese women's pitch movements which reached the utmost pitch levels. In the case of Japanese women, their pitch registers are comprised of elevated highest pitch levels (toplines). Their highest pitch levels sometimes reached above 400 Hz and occasionally 500 Hz while American women's highest pitch levels remained below 400 Hz. Figure 3.11 shows the pitch movements attaining utmost pitch levels adopted by Japanese and American women:

When Japanese women's pitch movements reaching the ultimate pitch levels were examined, it was found that they were not identical to their maximum pitch movements. By contrast, American female informants maximum pitch movements are *identical* to those which attained the utmost pitch levels (with the exception of one informant). This means that Japanese female informants' pitch movements reaching the ultimate pitch levels are narrower than their maximum pitch movements (except for one informant). Figure 3.12 compares Japanese female informants' pitch movements which attained the utmost pitch levels with their maximum pitch movements presented in the ERB-rate scale.

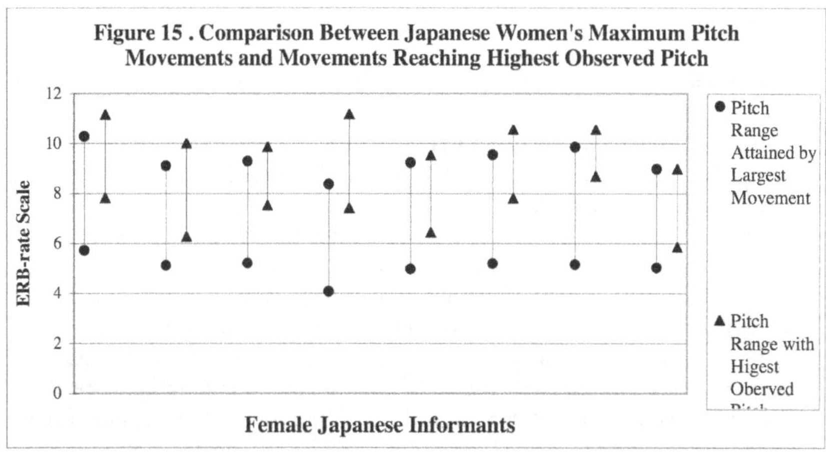

Figure 3.11 Maximum pitch range values as compared with median values obtained from Japanese and American informants

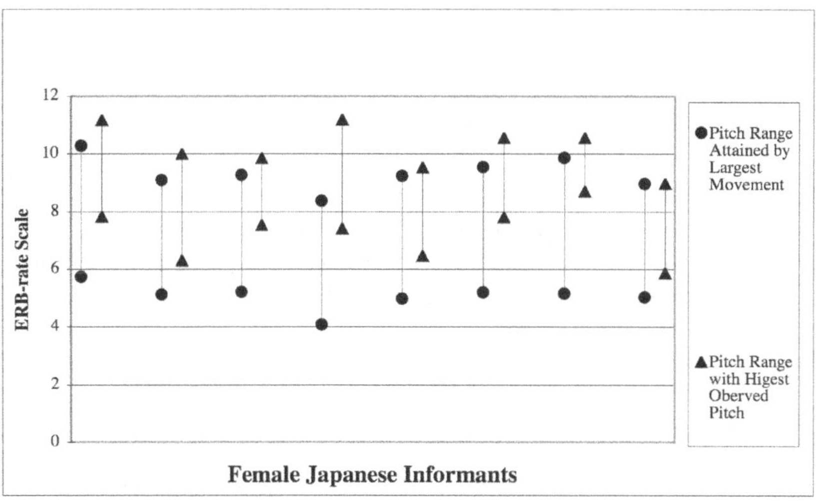

Figure 3.12 Comparison between Japanese women's maximum pitch movements and movements reaching highest observed pitch.

Notes

1. See the section of 'Perception of voice pitch (linear and non-linear logarithmic scales)' in this chapter.
2. Yamazawa and Hollien claim that the 'tone' aspect of Japanese could account for the addition of a group of higher frequencies to the SFF distributions, raising the overall SFF mean for these speakers.
3. Yamazawa and Hollien derived this inference based on their discovery that most Japanese female informants exhibited bimodal frequency distribution patterns. This finding was essentially a confirmation of Vance's (1986) and Yamazawa's (1987) studies (cited in Yamazawa and Hollien, 1992) each reporting their Japanese subjects tendency to exhibited bimodal SFF distributions. Vance detected the bimodal SFF distribution with double peaks on a normal distribution pattern. An additional mini-peak at the higher end on a skewed distribution characterizes the bimodal SFF distribution uncovered by Yamazawa. This propensity was markedly different from that of the unimodal patterns observed for Americans. Yamazawa and Hollien concluded that this speaking characteristic is language specific: the pitch accent element within Japanese accounts for the Japanese women's bimodal SFF distribution patterns.
4. The following is the list of the topics with which the informants were engaged in each conversation.

    1. The conversations the informants held with the vice president. (M: Male; F: Female)

M1: motorcycles	F1: host family
M2: apartment	F2: English classes
M3: golf	F3: host family
M4: host family	F4: host family

    2. The conversations the informants held with each other

M1 and M2: motorcycles	F1 and F2: vacation
M3 and M4: sleeping	F3 and F4: laundry and roommates

5. See the section of 'Perception of voice pitch (linear and non-linear logarithmic scales)' in this chapter.
6. The short-term average F0 values are obtained by counting the number of cycles of the fundamental within the averaging interval (50 ms) from the oscillogram and multiplying that number by 20 (50 ms = 1/20 s) (Jassem, 1971: 60).
7. In 1999, I examined the potential effects of interlocutors' gender on voice pitch usage in Japanese male speakers' speech data in my preliminary study. It was found that there was no effect. Moreover, I was not able to identify any clear pattern as to how the interlocutors' sex might have influenced the width of pitch movements utilized by informants in my comparative study.

4   Voice Pitch and Expression of Emotion

In this chapter I examine the meanings of voice pitch modulation in terms of a universal human behavior: the expression of emotion. I found this human behavior crucial in the understanding of the differences in voice pitch modulation used by speakers of Japanese and American English. The chapter initially introduces research on the nature of emotion conducted in the field of psychology as well as linguistic approaches to the role of intonation in expressing emotion. It considers theories of emotion as well as cross-cultural studies on facial expressions of emotion. The chapter then turns to Doi's discussion (1981) of two Japanese psychological concepts of self-indulgence (*amae*) and restraint (*enryo*), which will eventually be incorporated into my interpretation of politeness as it relates to voice pitch modulation in the following chapter. I integrate the *uchi* (inner)/*soto* (outer) orientation of Japanese society into this discussion. The chapter proceeds, next, to research about roles intonation (pitch modulation): grammatical, discursive, 'focus structure,' and acoustical perspectives. Of the four viewpoints which are introduced in this chapter, only acoustical approach is solely concerned with emotional meaning of the intonation. Nevertheless, I found the perspective of 'focus structure' useful in comprehending intonation's meaning in general. The chapter closes with a discussion of how degree of emotional involvement can be correlated with voice pitch movement width for my comparative investigation.

Expression of Emotion

One's understanding of emotion is probably universal, since most people believe that they already know a great deal about the subject (Plutchik, 1980: 4). People believe that emotions are strong inner impulses that influence thoughts and behaviors. Those emotions seemingly are not within our control or mastery. We know that some emotions feel pleasant and others unpleasant. We also know that some people are more emotional than others. Clearly, our understanding of emotion is still developing and is infinitely more complex a notion than would appear.

Concepts of Emotion

From a historical point of view, psychologists regard Charles Darwin the first major proponent of ideas about the nature of emotion (Plutchik and Kellerman, 1980: xv). According to Plutchik and Kellerman, Darwin acclaimed that the concept of evolution applied to the behavior and 'emotion' of animals not only to the evolution of physical constructions. Darwin's book, *The Expression of the Emotions in Man and Animals* (published in 1872), includes a large body of anecdotal and observational evidence regarding the expression of emotions in lower animals, preliterate human groups, infants, and Western Europeans. With this evidence he eventually arrived at certain important conclusions. Darwin determined that emotions have evolved with specific functions, primarily to increase the likelihood of survival of a given species. These functions of emotion are to help predict the possible behavior and prepare an animal for appropriate response. Emotions for Darwin are essentially adaptive. They help coordinate an animal's behavior in a way that is suitable to its environmental conditions (Plutchik and Kellerman 1980: xvi).

Traditional Views in Western Psychology

In 1922 James and Lange proposed what has become a highly influential one of the oldest theories of emotion in Western psychology. Their theory suggested that the conscious experience of emotion arises from one's perception of 'autonomic arousal' and apparent behavior. Thus, when you see a bear and consequently run away, your interpretation of your running (with the accompanying fast respiration and heart rate) generates the emotional experience of fear.

> My theory is that the bodily changes follow directly the perception
> of the exciting fact, and that our feeling of the same changes as
> they occur in the emotion. (Lange and James, 1922: 100)

However, two other theorists, Cannon (1927) and Bard (1934) argued *contra*. For them, 'autonomic arousal' was not a satisfactory explanation – it was simply not fast enough to account for changes in emotional experience. They suggested that emotional experience resulted from direct stimulation of brain centers in the cortex which caused the conscious experience of emotion (D. Matsumoto, 1996: 117).

More recently, Schachter and Singer (1962) focused on the role of cognitive interpretation (Crawford, Kippax, Onyx, Gault and Benton, 1992: 21; D. Matsumoto, 1996: 117). Their theory holds that emotional incitement or behavior need not be differentiated according to 'autonomic arousal' or behavior. For them, one's interpretation of the environment in which one is being 'emotionally triggered' is important in the production of conscious emotional experience. Emotion therefore arises from the marking (onset) of the arousal or behavior in that situation.

Other important theories of emotion advocated by such psychologists as Tomkins, Izard, Plutchik, and Ekman focus on the aspect of its expression (Crawford *et al.*, 1992: 19; D. Matsumoto, 1996: 117). These theories generally argue that emotions are evolutionarily adaptive. Thus their expression is biologically innate and universal to people of all cultures and races. These academicians confirmed their perspectives by quoting research documenting universal expressions and recognition of facial expressions of emotion.

D. Matsumoto (1996: 117–18), whose work will be discussed at a later point in this chapter, addresses the following view concerning the meaning of emotion in American culture. What is common among these diverse theoretical views is that emotion has an immense personal and individual meaning in Western psychology and culture. American psychology views inner, subjective feeling as the primary defining characteristic of emotion. Americans esteem the feelings of people including those of children, and make special efforts to take into account those feelings when making major decisions. The main purpose of understanding emotion is to help define one's unique individuality; one's self-definitions. That is, one's emotions influence the ways in which one defines and identifies oneself because they are personal and private expressions for Americans.

Understanding Emotions in Japan

In contrasting how the Japanese deal with their emotions, D. Matsumoto (1996: 123) argues that for the Japanese people, emotions do not bear the personal, individual importance they receive in the American culture. Rather, individual feelings and reflection are meaningful more in the sense of one's relationship to *society* and to everyday social interactions. The Japanese concept of *amae* (which will be discussed at a later point in this chapter), for example, refers to an interdependent *relation-ship* between two individuals, not a special emotion with its meaning attached only to one person. Emotion is important in the Japanese culture not because of its intense, personal meanings for oneself. It is important because of its implications for one's *relationships* with others and how those relationships may vary in the future. For instance, joy or happiness, according to Matsumoto, is not solely an expression of inner felicity for the Japanese. Rather, the emotion may be attached to the successful outcome or consequence of one's *relationship with others* (such as the successful accomplishment of certain social obligations).

Cross-cultural Research on Universality of Emotional Expression

In 1872 Charles Darwin argued that emotional reactions, particularly facial and vocal expressions are also innate and thus universal for at least some basic, distinct emotions such as joy, sadness, fear, and anger (Matsumoto, Kuhdo, Scherer, and Wallbott, 1988: 21). As a pioneer in the field of the psychology of emotion, his work eventually culminated in a sustained debate between 'universalists' and advocates of the 'culture specific view' of emotional expression (Ekman, 1973).

LaBarre (1947; 1962) and Birdwhistell (1970) described cultural differences in emotional behavior. This commentary received wide attention and was generally accepted as evidence that facial behavior linked with emotion was socially learned and thus culturally mutable (D. Matsumoto, 1996: 22). However, these researchers, Matsumoto argues, lacked quantitative evidence. They mainly relied on anecdotal perceptions, descriptions by novelists, and anthropological reports, in support of a culture-specific view of emotional expression. Nevertheless, their theory became more generally accepted than that of Darwin's over time.

Ekman, Friesen, and Izard provided some of the earliest evidence for cultural universals of expressions of emotion. In one of their studies, Ekman and Friesen (1971) photographed various facial expressions depicting emotion and took those pictures to five different countries (the United States, Japan, Chile, Argentina, and Brazil). They asked people in each of these countries to label the emotion they thought was being expressed on a face. They found that the informants correctly identified six emotions with consistently high agreement across all five cultures. In the same year, Izard (1971) conducted his study independently but according to the same methodological procedures. The study generated exactly the same findings.

Some researchers have argued that 'shared visual input' *vis-à-vis* American mass media and movies could have influenced the results of Ekman's and Friesen's study. That is, the outcome of their study simply confirmed that people in other cultures *already* intuitively understood the significance of emotional expressions depicted by Americans in photographs shown to them. Ekman's and Friesen's became a subject of great criticism. In order to rebut to these criticisms, they subsequently conducted their studies in two preliterate tribal cultures in New Guinea. These tribes had very little contact with the Western world. Thus, 'shared visual input' could not possibly explain cultural agreement in evaluations or expressions of emotion. They confirmed that the New Guinea tribal people interpreted facial stimuli in exactly the same manner as did informants in earlier studies. They also asked the New Guineans to model various emotions on their faces. They then showed videotapes of these expressions to American observers, who were asked to evaluate which emotions were being depicted. In spite of the fact that none of the Americans had ever seen or had any kind of contact with New Guineans, they were nevertheless able to accurately judge which emotions were being portrayed (Ekman and Friesen, 1971).

Ekman and Friesen also examined the actual expressions which people from different cultures exhibited when emotions were provoked. They compared the spontaneous emotional reactions of Japanese with American informants. In this study (Ekman, 1972; Friesen, 1972), people from both cultures watched intense, stress-inducing films in a laboratory. The films included scenes of a burn, an amputation, childbirth with forceps, and an aboriginal puberty rite. Their facial expressions, recorded by a hidden video camera, were then coded through the medium of a facial measurement technique known as the Facial Affect Scoring Technique (FAST). FAST decomposed the expressions that occurred into their most basic units. Comparative components exhibited by the Japanese displayed exactly the same expression components of emotion as the Americans at precisely the same moments of the film. In other words, all viewers' responses were identical.

Ekman and Friesen at this point proposed a theory which accounts for the foregoing findings. They argue persuasively the existence of a biologically innate Facial Affect Program which retains the facial prototypes of universal emotions in the brain. They believe that seven universal facial expressions (anger, contempt, disgust, fear, happiness, sadness, surprise) are biologically innate and occur identically for all people, regardless of race, culture, or gender. When the emotion is triggered, a signal is transmitted to the Facial Affect Program. This program then transmits a message to one's face to express the emotion. After additional studies (e.g., Ekman *et al.*, 1987; Matsumoto and Ekman, 1989) that confirmed the earlier findings, universality of emotional expressions is no longer debated in academic circles (D. Matsumoto, 1996: 26).

Cross-cultural Research on Emotion and Japan

Ekman, a world-renowned leader of research and theory in the field of human emotion, and his collaborator, Friesen, were both interested in cross-cultural research which included that done in Japan. However, D. Matsumoto is the researcher who concentrated on examining *Japanese* emotional behaviors in the field of psychology. Since the mid-1980s he has conducted research under the auspices of Ekman and Friesen. The content of the following six sections were selected mainly from D. Matsumoto's 1996 synopsis of his and his collaborators' findings with regard to Japanese emotion.

Japanese People and Facial Expressions

The aforementioned studies performed by Ekman and Friesen in 1972 included another condition involving the same participants. In the second part of the study, each of the participants viewed the stress-triggering stimuli again, but this time in the *presence* of a higher-status experimenter. In order to clarify the status difference between the participants and the researcher, the experimenter was an older male who wore clothes suitable to his status – shirt, slacks, tie, and white lab coat. As the participants watched the films, the experimenter sat in front of them, taking in their facial responses. As before, their facial behaviors were videotaped without their knowledge and deciphered again through the FAST (Facial Affect Scoring Technique). Facial coding indicated that the Americans by and large still exhibited the identical negative emotions as they expressed in the first part of the experiment. However, the Japanese expressions were different. They differed not only from the Americans' but also from their own emotional reactions in the earlier experiment. In every instance in which the Americans showed negative emotions, the Japanese either showed no emotion or simply smiled.

Ekman and Friesen suggested that the differences in facial displays occurring in the second part of their experiment derive from cultural differences in display rules. Display rules are the rules that people learn early in life to manipulate their facial expressions of emotion, depending on social environment (Ekman and Friesen, 1969). The Japanese apparently follow the display rule which tells them to conceal negative feelings in the presence of someone with higher status. This rule forced them to mask their negative feelings with a smile. Since the Americans have no such display rule in their cultural repertory, they exhibited basically the identical expression as before.

Japanese People and Emotional Experiences: Evaluation of the Emotion-eliciting Situations

In their 1988 report, Matsumoto *et al.* described a large-scale cross-cultural study on emotional experience. The informants were asked to report on three evaluative aspects of their most recent emotion-inducing incident. The three issues were: '1) the antecedents and determinants of emotion; 2) the reactions of the informants; and 3) the amount of control and coping attempts' (Matsumoto *et al.*, 1988: 7).

The study involved eight European countries including Israel, the United States, and Japan. A strong degree of similarity of the data from different cultures was observed, supporting the notion of universal and biologically based differences between individual emotions. At the same time, however, much of the data also distinguishes Japanese experience from that of European and American (which tends to be more similar). Japanese informants reported fewer cases of visible expressions of joy, fewer cases of sadness resulting from death and separation, less 'stranger-elicited fear' but much more 'stranger-elicited anger', and fewer cases of anger caused by perceived injustice (Matsumoto *et al.*, 1988: 26–30).

As far as the intensity and duration of emotional experience are concerned, the Japanese reported that they felt the emotion for shorter periods of time and less powerfully, compared to American responses (Matsumoto *et al.*, 1988: 17–20). However, there was no difference in the response between the Japanese informants and their European and other counterparts. The actual scale values indicated that the Japanese had a tendency to report on the higher end of the scale as opposed to the lower. Moreover, when the issue of how frequently they experienced emotions was examined (Matsumoto *et al.*, 1988: 15), the Japanese perception was that each emotion had been experienced more recently than reported by Americans or Europeans. This suggests that each of the emotions is experienced with greater frequency for the Japanese than for the Europeans and Americans. It also implies that the Japanese accord greater significance to their emotions than non-Japanese. They may possibly ponder more about their emotions, remember them longer, and relegate greater importance to them than non-Japanese (D. Matsumoto, 1996: 67–8).

The informants were asked to discuss their reactions to the emotion-eliciting situations (Matsumoto *et al.*, 1988: 21–5). The Japanese reported less verbalization, less expressive behavior, and fewer physiological sensations than their American and European counterparts. This result is in accordance with the aforementioned study on display rules and facial expressions of emotion. It is also consistent with stereotypical notions of the Japanese as 'inscrutable Orientals,' hiding emotions behind expressionless or polite smiling faces. This means that despite the fact that Japanese do experience subjective emotions as much as Europeans and Americans, they do not react as palpably as Europeans and Americans.

The informants were also asked whether or not they were consciously trying to control or regulate their emotional reactions. The Japanese reported that they controlled their verbal or nonverbal expressive reactions (or physiological symptoms and sensations) in a similar degree as the Americans and Europeans. D. Matsumoto speculates that the Japanese, from an early age, must have learned and mastered their cultural display rules such that their reactions are automatically controlled without any conscious effort. The Japanese do not view themselves as self-policing their behavior because it is simply part of their cultural disposition – part of being Japanese and part of being their normal selves. D. Matsumoto emphasizes that the Western presumption which holds that the Japanese control their emotional expressions is simply a culturally biased view of how the Japanese manage their emotions (D. Matsumoto 1996: 26).

Feeling Rules and Japanese Culture

Since emotion is a universal phenomenon, as the aforementioned research has demonstrated, the Japanese have many of the same kinds of emotional reactions with the same kinds of subjective feelings as people all over the world. However, emotion functions to bind members of the society together in Japanese culture; that is, sharing emotions is a *communal* effort. In this community of spirit, empathy is an important psychological value in a culture where individualism is downplayed. The emotions function to maintain the insular and strongly interpersonal nature of Japanese society (D. Matsumoto, 1996: 74).

'Feeling rules,' a term coined by Hochshild, are useful in considering the specific ways in which cultures regulate subjective emotional experience (D. Matsumoto, 1996: 75). They are culturally and socially derived rules which decide when and how an individual experiences emotion. D. Matsumoto borrowed Hochshild's concept of feeling rules applying its tenets to Japanese culture. His interpretation of the rules is that in Japan they operate so automatically that no conscious control or decision is necessary on the individual's part (D. Matsumoto, 1996: 76). The evidence is that the Japanese reported that they did not in fact control or regulate their emotional experiences. Moreover, they clearly had less response both physically and mentally to presenting emotions than their Western counterparts.

Individualism-collectivism and Status Differentiation Influence on Emotion in Japan as a Function of In-group and Out-group

Using the theoretical frameworks of IC (Individualism-Collectivism) and in-group and out-group distinction, D. Matsumoto suggests that cultural differences in IC would produce variations in the display of emotion as a function of ingroups and outgroups. In comparison with individualistic cultures, members of collective ones would display more positive emotions to ingroups because of the culture's greater pressure to maintain harmony within those structures. At the same time, they would exhibit more *negative* emotions to outgroups.

However, members of high SD (Status Differentiation) cultures would display more positive emotions to higher-status individuals with more negative emotions shown to lower-status ones. The demonstration of positive emotions to higher-status parties would act as signals of appeasement and deference. On the other hand, the exhibition of negative emotions to lower-status parties would function to maintain one's own higher status. When considering Eastern-Western cultural differences, these ideas are well-suited to understanding cultural similarities and differences in the emotions of the Japanese (D. Matsumoto, 1996: 137–45).

A study alluded to earlier in this chapter on display rules supports many of these ideas concerning IC and SD influences on emotion in Japan. As part of this study, Americans and Japanese participants were asked how appropriate they thought it would be to express the universal emotions (as conceptualized by Ekman and Fresen) in eight differing situations. These eight circumstances refer to when one is: (1) alone; (2) with family; (3) with friends; (4) with casual acquaintances; (5) in public; (6) with people of lower status than oneself; (7) with people of higher status than oneself; and (8) with children (D. Matsumoto, 1996: 145).

The Japanese felt that the showing of anger and fear was a more appropriate response with casual acquaintances and in a public place. D. Matsumoto's reasoning for this outcome is that the collectivist Japanese culture differentiates more between ingroups and outgroups than the individualistic society, thus allowing for the expression of negative emotions to ougroups. Similarly, the Japanese thought that anger was more appropriate to people of lower status than did the Americans (individualists) since the status-differentiating Japanese culture requires the maintenance of status differences much more than the (individualistic) American one. Likewise, the Japanese felt that fear was more appropriate to show to people of higher status presumably because that fear was motivated by feelings of deference toward such individuals (D. Matsumoto, 1996: 145–8).

Individualism-collectivism and Status Differentiation Influences on Japanese Display Rules

The Japanese display rules of emotions are directly linked to IC and SD because, according to Matsumoto, they either '1) maintain harmony and cohesion within ingroups, and to differentiate outgroups; or 2) maintain status differences among high-, low-, and same-status others' (D. Matsumoto, 1996: 148).

When interacting with other members of their group, the Japanese must ensure that the harmony of the group is not threatened by dangerous emotions so that the intrinsic peace of that community is not jeopardized. The sharing of emotional expression and experience, on the other hand, strengthens bonds among group members. It is more acceptable for a higher-status person to show anger to lower-status individuals than vice versa. A person of lower-status must exhibit emotions so as to reinforce an awareness of the difference in status. This parallels the way in which a higher-status party, to maintain status differences, demonstrates anger toward those occupying a lower station.

Japanese Psychology (of *Amae* and *Enryo*)

Doi (1973: 36–41), a Japanese psychiatrist, discusses the relation between *amae* and *enryo*. Based on his clinical experience, he argues that these psychological concepts are peculiar to Japanese culture. *Enryo* arguably meant 'thoughtful consideration.' The literal meaning of the two characters translates to *en* (distance) and *ryo* (consideration). It is roughly equivalent to 'restraint' or 'holding back.' For Doi, it is mainly used as 'a negative yardstick in measuring the intimacy of human relationships' (Doi, 1973: 38). In the parent–child relationship there is no *enryo* and the relationship is permeated with *amae*. In this case, neither the child nor the parents feel *enryo* towards each other. In other relationships, the degree of *enryo* decreases proportionately with intimacy and increases with distance.

Amae, on the other hand, is 'self-indulgence' (Doi, 1973: 29). Doi (1973: 72) sees the ultimate example of *amae* in an infant's behavior with its mother. If A is said to be *amai* (the adjective form) to B, it means that s/he allows B to behave self-indulgently, presuming the existence of a special relationship (Doi, 1973: 29). B, therefore, is also allowed to release his or her feelings and emotions freely (at least to a certain degree). The most natural relationship in which *amae* plays a critical role, according to Doi, is that of the parent and child. *Amae* also comes into play in the relationships that are quasi-parental in nature. As mentioned earlier, D. Matsumoto argues that emotion is important in Japanese culture because of its implications for *relationships* between people rather than as the individual experience of a particular person. I believe that this line of reasoning only partially applies to this situation. I speculate that in the relationship in which *amae* exists, the person who is allowed to be self-indulged is also permitted to experience a more spontaneous release or expression of personal emotion. In addition, in this circumstance, the self-indulgent act of one person may be experienced positively by other people.

On the other hand, in the relationship where *enryo* is prevalent, such a personal experience of spontaneous expression of emotion is not tolerated. The Japanese person 'holds back' (i.e., refrains from expressing emotions or desires) with the idea that one must not presume too much upon the other's good will. The apparent fear is that unless one holds back, one will be thought disrespectful and therefore disliked. Therefore, generally speaking, *enryo* is felt to be confining and detested as such; nonetheless it retains its value. 'The presence or absence of *enryo* is used by the Japanese as a yardstick' for distinguishing between the types of human relationships that the Japanese refer to as 'inner' and 'outer' (Doi, 1973: 39).

The Japanese have linked this pair of concepts of inner *(uchi)* and outer *(soto)* with a set of meanings of self and society respectively. In the past, the concept has been discussed by researchers in anthropology such as Bachnik, Charles, and Quinn (1994). At the outermost pole, the Japanese are self-disciplined, detaching themselves from personal feelings. At the innermost pole, they are free to express ideas and feelings in a more individualistic sense. In this Japanese orientation to social life, the outer pole represents more distant, authoritative human relations. The inner pole, in contrast, represents more intimate, spontaneous relationships.

Lebra (1976) notes that in a situation where a Japanese individual defines the other (or both) as an outsider, s/he is afraid that the other party might exert her/his influence in various ways depending on her/his own conduct. In this situation s/he controls his/her expressions and emotions since direct self-exposure is far too dangerous. S/he physically and emotionally maintains a distance through this required behavioral restraint from another (Lebra, 1976: 120–1). Lebra here is alluding to the working of *enryo* in the outer circle of the Japanese society.

Emotion and Intonation (Pitch Modulation)

I now turn to the topic of what kind of research approaches have been taken to comprehend our voice pitch modulation in terms of intonation (pitch modulation) that we use in our speech. I consider how these approaches are relevant to expressing our attitudes and feelings. I then elucidate how I interpret the correlation between the width of voice pitch movements and demonstration of emotion.

Intonation is viewed as being the main medium of affective information (Ladd, 1980). Four approaches taken by researchers to understand intonational functions are grammatical, discourse-centered, 'focus structure', and acoustic. The acoustic approach is directly concerned with the role of intonation in expressing emotional states. By contrast, the grammatical and discourse-centered approaches have less emphasis on the attitudinal functions of intonation. More recently, Lambrecht has explored the focus (Information) structure component of intonation. I describe this last approach to interpreting intonation in some details as I find it useful in explaining the distribution of pitch movements found in my speech data.

Role of Intonation

Grammatical Approach to Intonation

Advocates of the grammar-based approaches, like Armstrong and Ward, Pike, and Halliday believed that an utterance's intonation was dependent on specific grammatical facts about the utterance. This outlook on intonation aimed to do is to correlate intonation contours with various grammatical sentence-types ('question intonation,' 'declarative intonation,' and 'sentence-final intonation'). Exceptions are treated as depicting attitudinal (emotional) modifications (such as 'uninterested,' 'polite,' 'surprised,' etc.).

The research of Armstrong and Ward in 1926 led them to a conclusion that melodies of English sentences can be grouped into two types: Tune I and Tune II. Tune I speech with final falling pitch is said to occur in 'ordinary' statement (i.e. 'They came to call yesterday afternoon'). Similarly, it was used in questions requiring a response other than 'yes' or 'no' as well as in commands and in exclamations (8ff). Tune II with final rising pitch corresponds with 'indefinite' statements as well as questions requiring a 'yes' or 'no' answer, requests, and incomplete statements (Armstrong and Ward, 1926: 19ff).

In 1945 Pike contributed to the grammatical study of the role of intonation by arguing for the idea of four pitch phonemes for English intonation. These were extra-high (1), high (2), mid (3) and low (4) (Pike, 1945: 26). A falling contour to pitch level 4 (low) is seen as having the meaning of finality. A contour which descends to pitch level 3 (mid) is felt to be incomplete and suggestive of an addition (Pike, 1945: 45). A falling terminal contour from pitch level 1 (extra high) is seen as being more acutely persistent. This contour might have an element of surprise in contrast to a falling terminal contour from level 3 (mid), which is allegedly much milder and detached (Pike, 1945: 47f).

Halliday, however, did not hold with the idea of segmenting intonation into pitch phonemes. Instead he focused his research efforts in 1967 on the idea of a tone-group boundary. Halliday (1967: 36) posited that the presence or absence of the tone-group boundary would transform a sentence with one 'information unit' into a sentence with two 'information units.' He also argued in support of the idea that the variable location of tonic prominence would result in different 'information foci' (Halliday, 1967: 38). Halliday (1967: 41) reasoned that substituting rising for falling pitch on a tonic syllable would change a statement into a question. Still, his argument ran along the line that intonation is grammatical in function because such choices were 'systematically and distinctively related to meaning' (Couper-Kuhlen and Selting, 1996: 19).

Discourse Approach to Intonation

More recent theory of discourse intonation based on naturally occurring speech data seeks discourse rather than grammatical functions. In the early 1980s Brazil introduced the idea of two distinctive tones for English discourse (Brazil, 1980; Brazil, Coulthard, and Johns, 1981). The first one that falls and then rises was termed a 'referring' tone. The second one that simply falls was a 'proclaiming' tone. He noted that the falling-rising tone referred 'to a piece of information as part of the common ground, the falling tone to proclaim a piece of information as new' (Brazil *et al.*, 1981: 13). He also brought forth the idea of three 'keys.' These were High, Mid and Low, which referred to the tones and functioned to describe their relative pitch height within the speaker's voice range. Brazil argued that Low key is said to 'mark an "equivalence" relation between items in successive tone groups while High key marks a "contrast" between two items' (Brazil *et al.*, 1981: 30). The notions of tone and key were responsible at least in some part for the distinctive oppositions occurring in English discourse.

The Concept of Focus (Information) Structure Component of Intonation

Ladd in 1980 observed, 'focus is signaled solely by the location of the accent; various intonational characteristics such as greater volume and widened pitch range can also be used to signal what might be called "emphasis"' (Ladd, 1980: 213). Lambrecht (1996: 5) calls this type of focus 'expressive use' of intonation for understanding speakers' attitudes toward propositions.[1] Lambrecht commenced his discussion on the information (focus) structure[2] component of intonation by invoking Bolinger's definition of the 'information point' of a sentence. He did this in an effort to give a functional account of sentence accentuation. Bolinger (1954: 152) elaborated that the point of the sentence marked by prosodic stress is where 'there is a greatest concentration of information, that which the hearer would be less likely to infer without being told.' Lambrecht diverged in his thinking from Bolinger's view at this point. He held that:

> certain prosodic phenomena which have been subsumed under general concept of 'focus' is related to marking of different 'activation[3] states' of discourse referents[4], which in turn serves to indicate certain 'topic[5] discontinuities' in the discourse. (Lambrecht, 1996: 208)

For Lambrecht 'focus' is 'the semantic component of a pragmatically structured proposition whereby the assertion[6] differs from the presupposition[7] '(Lambrecht, 1996: 213). The general discourse function of all sentence accents is expressed by him as:

> A sentence accent indicates an instruction from the speaker to the hearer to establish a pragmatic relation between a denotatum[8] and a proposition holds. (Lambrecht, 1996: 325)

Lambrecht differentiates between two major kinds of accents: focus and topic accents:

> Focus accent: An activation accent which marks the denotatum of the accented constituent as entering a focus relation with the proposition. It marks it as the element whose presence makes a proposition into an assertion. (Lambrecht, 1996: 325)

Topic accent: An activation accent which marks the referent of the accent constituent entering a topic relation with the proposition, i.e., as being the element which the proposition will be about or which serves to establish the temporal, spatial, instrumental framework within the proposition holds (Lambrecht, 1996: 325).

Lambrecht highlighted the difference between focus and topic accent in an example borrowed from Ladd (Lambrecht, 1996: 327):

> (13) (a) A: Hey, (you) come HERE.
> (b) B: No, YOU come HERE.

In B's response to A, the emphasis on YOU establishes the role of the referent as the topic of the proposition. Therefore, it is deemed a topic accent. The accent is necessary since the referent of the topic expression YOU is different from the understood topic 'you' in A's statement. In contrast, the accent on HERE in B's reply is denoted as focus accent. The accent is imperative because its omission would 'mark the designatum of the open proposition 'x comes here' as pragmatically presupposed' (Lambrecht, 1996: 327).

Interpretations of the Relationship Between Emotion and Intonation (Pitch Modulation)

I clearly observe all the aforementioned approaches to intonation. However, as Bolinger emphasizes, I believe in intonation's emotional contribution (Bolinger, 1986: 195–7) and its independence from lexico-syntax (Bolinger, 1989: 1). Bolinger further maintains that the role of intonation is enormously important to concept of grammar. A speaker who produces an intonation reacts to feeling or attitude more directly than to any other aspects of spoken language (Bolinger 1986: viii). As emotion is always present, 'ideas are communicated symbolically through the feelings that manifest those ideas' (Bolinger, 1986: viii).

Bolinger's initial argument is that the listener is aware of pitch (which speech makes use of) in a dimension of tune or melody. The overall tune or melody in general creates impressions of mood or emotion (Bolinger, 1986: 9). Within the melody, certain conspicuous movements are used to make individual syllables stand out. These movements (or type of prominence) are achieved through the use of pitch. Secondly, the speaker, according to Bolinger, is not ordinarily capable of controlling the pitch of intonation. How she generates the melody as a whole and how much her pitch jumps to mark the accents often exceeds her own expectations in normal discourse (Bolinger, 1986: 13). Bolinger calls this the effect of emotion. He elaborates: 'With excitement there are greater extremes of pitch; with depression the range is narrowed' (Bolinger, 1986: 13).

By referring to accent cued by pitch, Bolinger asserts that pitch is the most heavily relied on prosodic feature in identifying accent. He argues that pitch is the most efficient cue – a long series of experiments starting with those of Dennis Fry in 1955 validated the precedence of pitch cues for accent (as against duration and loudness) (Bolinger 1986: 22). Further, in discussing the relationship between intonation and grammar, Bolinger notes that while intonation is requisite to grammar, the grammatical functions of intonation are *secondary* to emotional functions. Pitch changes manifested in feelings serve as prompts to alert listeners as to how speakers are feeling. He provides evidence for the immediately preceding argument by stating that speakers seldom contemplate their choice of an intonation pattern. Simply stated, they do not pause and ask themselves 'Which form would be best here for my purpose?' Instead, they identify the feeling they wish to convey and their intonation is automatically triggered by that feeling (Bolinger, 1986: 27).

As Bolinger (1986: 233) noted, the line between grammatical and affective uses of intonation is somewhat cloudy. For instance, one quickly discovers cases where the force of falling and rising final pitch used in both declarative and interrogative statements can be mostly 'emotional'. This might occur in a situation where falling pitch reveals impatience or insistence in yes-no type questions (Ladd, 1980: 105):

(14) (a) A: Did he finish?
     (b) B: Well, he's over at the grad school office right now, and ...

(c) A: Yeah, but did he finish?

Alternatively, we find an example of rising pitch which subliminal message is hesitation or deference in Lakoff's example (1975: 17):

(15) (a) Husband: What time is dinner?

(b) Wife: Six o'clock?

Grammatical contrasts have simultaneously 'emotional' functions clearly as the foregoing examples disclose. On of my efforts in this volume is to make persuasive interpretations for the socio-cultural meaning of wider and narrower voice pitch movements that I found in my data in terms of emotion. Thus, I found the findings of research employing the acoustic approach to the study of intonation (pitch modulation) most supportive of my study as it is directly concerned with types of emotion correlated with voice characteristics. I am indebted to the insights of such scholars as Uldall and Scherer on emotional meanings of intonation (pitch modulation)

Acoustical Approach

For researchers who advocated the acoustic approach, the first concern with the study of the role of intonation in expressing emotional state is to produce utterances that reliably and clearly convey certain affective messages (e.g., anger or surprise). This approach tries to identify acoustic features of the signal that usually occur when those messages are conveyed. The ultimate objective would be to locate correlations between perceptual judgment (which is experimentally obtained) and measured acoustic cues. Having speakers pronounce fixed texts with stimulated emotions (sometimes combined with speech synthesis) is a common method of securing utterances that convey specific affective messages. The accepted method of ascertaining what affective messages are conveyed by utterances is to have listeners rate the utterances on variety of judgment scales.

With these ideas as their methodological guidelines, numerous researchers investigated how acoustic features such as pitch is linked various types of emotion, as I documented in Chapter 2. In a 1986 review article, Scherer noted that most relevant and convincing finding, reported in all previous studies, was a consistent increase in mean F0, F0 range, and F0 variability of speech in the emotional conditions that can be classified as 'elation' (Scherer, 1986b: 161). Scherer provided further support for this pattern in his 1996 study. He found that mean F0 produced by the professional actors and actresses fell in the highest voice pitch range for the intense emotions such as 'elation.' Moreover, when a perception test was performed for recognition accuracy, the accuracy rates of boredom (76 percent) and interest (75 percent) were especially high.

In addition, results of cross-cultural perception tests involving Japanese, Europeans, and Americans performed on various types of emotion by and large have demonstrated better-than-chance accuracy in recognizing the types of emotion expressed. Most recently, Sakuraba, Imaizumi, and Kakehi (2004), who compared the acoustic features of voices produced by Japanese and American children, confirmed that elated emotions such as 'joy' are expressed with much wider voice pitch ranges than those used to express neutral emotion in both cultures. Their finding suggests that human voice pitch modulation may be universally related to emotion in many, if not all, cultures.

Distribution of Pitch Ranges

The following observations can be made, when examining the distribution of pitch ranges in my own data. In order to recognize a general intonation pattern which intonation groups form, it was necessary in many cases to ignore both filled and unfilled pauses. A series of intonation groups (IG), beginning with a widest pitch range, gradually decreasing in width and ending with a narrower pitch-range, generally seems to represent a clause or a sentence (simple or complex).

This syntactic unit (clause or sentence) can be also interpreted as a breath group[9] (Lieberman, 1967: 26). Lieberman defined the breath group as 'an expiration of air from the lungs, which has been claimed as a cause of downdrift.'[10] For example, in Japanese, the accent of the first minor phrase of a major phrase is achieved as high pitch; the accents of the subsequent minor phrases reach only mid level (McCawley, 1977). It was generally observed in my data that it is the initial IG within the breath group which appears to contribute to the difference in pitch range width utilized in conversations with interlocutors of different degrees of familiarity. The following drawing is illustrative of the ideas specified above.

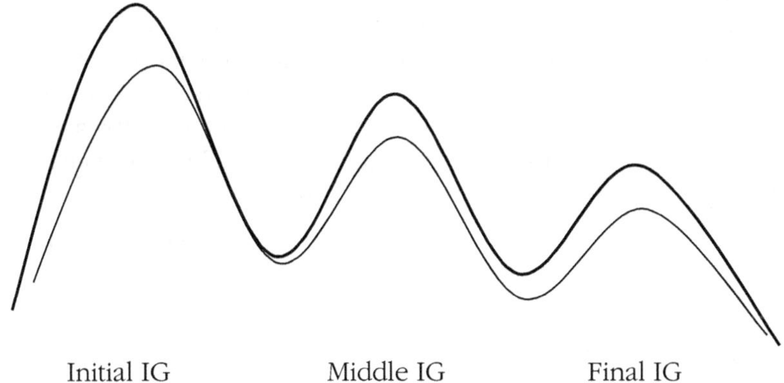

The pitch contour indicated in a thick solid line typically represents the width of ranges often used during conversations with a familiar interlocutor. By contrast, the pitch contour represented by a thin solid line demonstrates pitch-ranges employed by speakers when conversing with unfamiliar interlocutors. I believe that this difference in the pitch-range is the difference in expressiveness components of intonational meaning. The difference between the width of pitch ranges used in these two dissimilar conversations designates the difference in degree of emotions expressed in them.

However, on numerous occasions in spontaneous discourses, a noticeable increase in pitch range seems to occur at any location within the breath group. This can be an indication of a focus or topic accent and is closely related to both syntactic and semantic structure of the unit (which Lambrecht explicated). During the conversation held between a male informant and his interlocutor in the pilot study, he responses to the question asking his residency as shown in below:

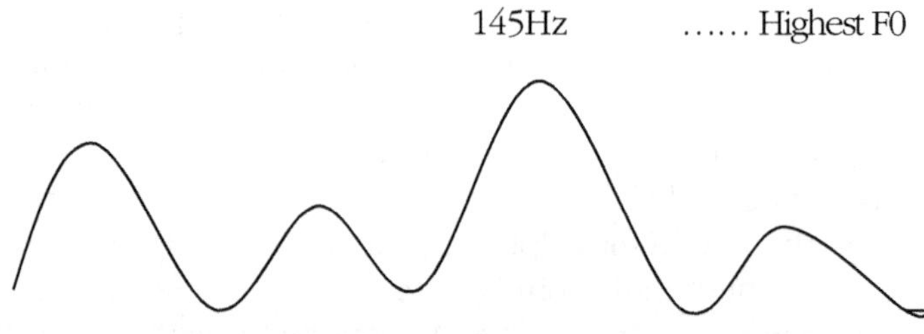

(16) Shinjuku kara densya de   hitotu   nandesu keredomo.
From Shinjuku by train   one (station) is + it is that

'It is that (My house) is <u>one</u> station away from Shinjuku by train….'

In the foregoing example, a wider pitch range marked by the prominent highest F0 (145?Hz) appears to be the case of the focus accent. Acccording to Lambrecht, this is precisely where the denotatum (*hitotu*) enters a focus relation with the proposition. A situation where topic accent occurs is seen in another example. The interlocutor asked the informant what he would be interested in doing as his future task in his company:

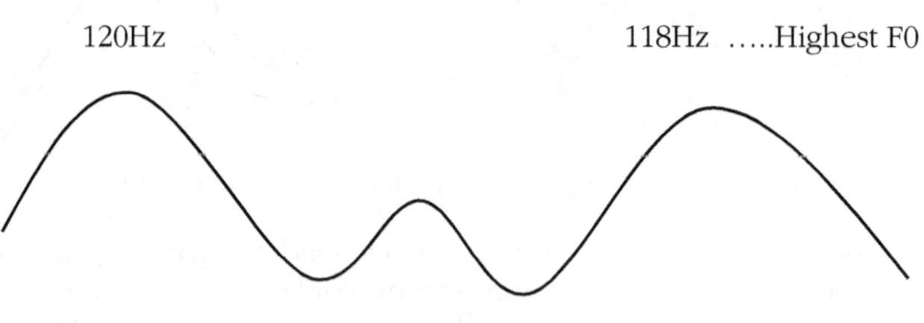

(17) Kojinteki niwa   toosi kankee o   <u>kiboo site imasu</u>.
personally   investment-related (work)   hoping

'Personally, (I) <u>am hoping</u> for investment -related (work).'

The verb referent (*koboo site iamsu*) has a topic accent, serving to establish itself as the topic, with respect to the proposition, which is to be interpreted as relevant information. This topic accent is manifested in the wider pitch-range as expressed with the highest F0 of 120Hz. Similarly, the omitted subject referent (*watasi* 'I') can be interpreted as another topic of this proposition. It is reflected in the adverbial phrase (*kojinteki niwa* 'personally'). The conspicuously wider pitch-range of 98?Hz displayed in the highest F0 of 118?Hz used to utter the adverb referent may signify a topic accent. Nevertheless, it appears me that this also expresses the speaker's strong personal desire (emotion or attitude) toward the proposition.

Emotion and Voice Pitch Movement Width

This book focuses on comparing the width of pitch movements used in all types of intonation contours. The investigation attempts to identify the relationship between the degree of emotional involvement or expression and the pitch range widths. Identifying specific emotions displayed in these pitch range widths is unfortunately outside the scope of the present investigation. Limiting the topic of conversation to 'food' controlled the degree of emotion (which the informants of the present study might exhibit). This topic was chosen because it is an emotionally non-provocative yet still remains an interesting subject for conversation.

As noted earlier, studies of emotion utilizing acoustic approach have confirmed a consistent increase in mean F0, F0 range, and F0 variability of speech in the emotional states identified as 'elation.' Bolinger (1989: 13) also stated that 'with excitement there are greater extremes of pitch; with depression the range is narrowed.' In the following two discourse analyses gleaned from the data in my comparative, increases in the width of pitch ranges which indicate heightened expressiveness of emotion, are observed. In the first example, a male informant, in conversing with an *unfamiliar* interlocutor, gives a report of an eccentric sushi restaurant he has been to. He is extremely amused by the types of sushi served here. Below, he expresses his amazement about the restaurant proprietor to his unfamiliar interlocutor:

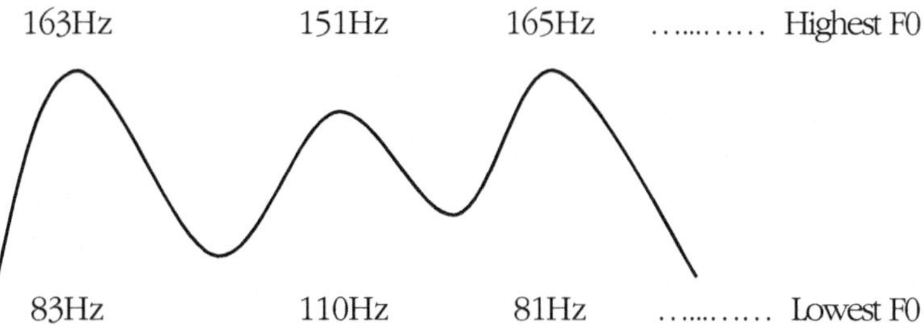

(18) *Oonaa wa   itioo   nihonjin   rasii ndesu yo.*
   the owner   at least a Japanese seem to be (I tell you)

'The owner seems to be a Japanese person, at least (I tell you).'

In another conversation, the same male informant describes the same restaurant to a *familiar* interlocutor:

205Hz   243Hz   297Hz   188Hz   …… Highest F0

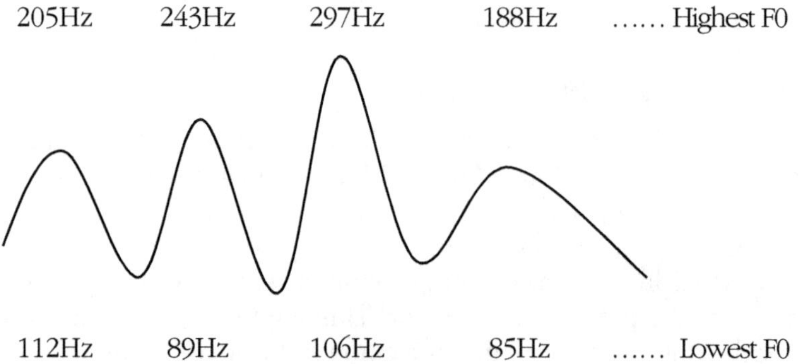

112Hz   89Hz   106Hz   85Hz   …… Lowest F0

(19) *Asoko no oonaa   nihonjin   mitai na   nda   kedo ne*
over there   the owner   a Japanese   seem to be   but (you know)

   'The owner over there seems to be a Japanese person, but (you know).'

In uttering a similar statement, this informant clearly differentiated in his usage of pitch movements. In the latter example, his pitch movements were much wider than those in the former example. This difference in the width of pitch movements is what this volume is most concerned with.

The above discourse analyses are presented here in order to interpret the differences in the voice pitch movement width exhibited in two situational variations by Japanese informants in my investigation. As noted earlier, in the relationship where *enryo* is prevalent such as the one existing in the utterance (18), spontaneous expression of emotion is suppressed. This suppression of expression of amazement is manifested in relatively narrow width of voice pitch excursions which the informant utilized in addressing an *unfamiliar* interlocutor. By contrast, the same informant exhibited an increase in the width of his voice pitch movements in displaying the same feeling of amazement when recounting his story to a *familiar* interlocutor, as in the utterance (19). This resulted from increases in his feelings of *amae* toward the familiar addressee. I, therefore, conclude that the amount of increases in the width of voice pitch movements displayed by Japanese speakers in conversing with familiar interlocutors is generally contingent upon the relative comfort of expressing their emotion based on the strength in the feelings of *amae*. I suspect that the similar phenomenon can possibly be observed among speakers in America (and also in other cultures). In the following chapter, I elucidate my findings of voice pitch width employed by American speakers in terms of politeness phenomena as it related to emphatic emotional expression.

As was reported in Chapter 3, when pitch movement measurements derived from conversations held between *familiar* interlocutors have been cross-culturally compared, it is generally found that the Japanese speakers adopt wider pitch movements than those of Americans. Does it ensue that Japanese speakers release more emotion than Americans do in conversing with familiar interlocutor? I would account for this discrepancy by considering the Japanese perspective of human orientation to the world that vacillates between two extremes: *Uchi* (inner) and *Soto* (outer). The Japanese have linked this pair of concepts of 'inner' (*uchi*) and 'outer' (*soto*) with a set of meanings of self and society respectively. In the past, the concept has been discussed by researchers in psychiatry and anthropology such as Doi, Bachnik, and Quinn. At the outermost pole, the Japanese are self-disciplined, detaching themselves from personal feelings. At the innermost pole, they are free to express ideas and emotions in a more individualistic sense. In this Japanese orientation to social life, the outer pole represents more distant, authoritative human relations. The inner pole, in contrast, represents more intimate, spontaneous relationships. Most Japanese consider it perfectly natural that a person should vary his/her way of relating to others depending on whether s/he is dealing with his/her inner circle or with the outer circle. They are expected to behave more spontaneously within their own circle yet control themselves outside it. In this culture it is critical to demonstrate the contrast in behavior according to the types of relationship a member of the society has with others. Thus, wider pitch movements (i.e., than Americans exhibited) adopted by Japanese informants are an example of the expected stance taken towards familiar interlocutors in their inner circle. This stance clearly contrasts with the stance taken toward unfamiliar interlocutors in the outer circle. In Japanese culture adopting wider pitch movements (than Americans do) in communicating with familiar interlocutors is apparently crucial for displaying and emphasizing one's willingness to share feelings within his/her 'inner circle.'

Notes

1.   'Conceptual representations of states of affairs' (Lambrecht, 1996: 5).
2.   'That component of sentence grammar in which propositions are paired with lexicogrammatical structures in accordance with the mental status of interlocutors who use and interpret these structures as units of information in given discourse contexts' (Lambrecht, 1996: 5).
3.   'To activate a referent is to establish a relation between the referent and a proposition, not simply to conjure up a representation of the referent in the mind of the addressee' (Lambrecht, 1996: 324).
4.   'The entities and states of affairs designated by linguistic expressions and the things designated by these expressions in particular utterance' (Lambrecht, 1996: 37).
5.   'A referent is interpreted as the topic of a proposition if in a given situation the proposition is construed as being about this referent, i.e. as expressing information which is relevant to and which increases the addressee's knowledge of this referent' (Lambrecht, 1996: 131).
6.   'The proposition expressed by a sentence which the hearer is expected to know or take for granted as a result of hearing the sentence uttered' (Lambrecht, 1996: 52).
7.   'The set of propositions lexicogrammatically evoked by a sentence which the speaker assumes the hearer already knows or ready to take for granted at the time the sentence is uttered' (Lambrecht, 1996: 52).
8.   'Expressions which designate attributes or relations of affairs, such as *small, in, went home*, etc.' (Lambrecht, 1996: 37).
9.   'A stretch of utterance produced within a single expiration of breath' (Crystal 1997: 48–9). The falling terminal fundamental frequency contour that results from the subglottal respiratory muscles lowering subglottal air pressure is a universal aspect of the (unmarked) breath group (Lieberman 1967: 104). The unmarked breath group boundaries were observed in Lieberman's data at the end of (simple) declarative sentences. The marked breath group represents increase in the tension of the laryngeal muscles during the last 150–200 msec of phonation, and thus has a terminal non-falling F0 contour. The marked breath group occurred in interrogative sentences in Lieberman's study.
10. Japanese utterances have been observed to involve a kind of natural downdrift, the mean pitch falls gradually from the beginning to the end of a syntactic unit such as a phrase or clause (Kawakami, 1977: 103–4; Higurashi, 1983: 87–90).

5   Voice Pitch, Politeness, and Gender

The other universal human behavior which I found essential in interpreting the differing voice pitch fluctuations employed by men and women in Japan and the United States is politeness. The concept will also be used to account for the outcome of my study presented in Chapter 3. Chapter 5 commences with a short introduction of the notion of politeness described by Lakoff, Brown and Levinson, and Ide. This section of the chapter also includes a summary of the prosodic features of politeness which Brown and Levinson observed. Further, Doi's discussion of Japanese psychology involving the notions of restraint (*enryo*) and self-indulgence (*amae*) will be brought forth again here. In Chapter 3, I demonstrated how these two concepts could explain the relation between Japanese speakers' degree of comfort in expressing their emotion and changes in their voice pitch movement width. In this chapter, I show that combining these psychological and cultural concepts with the notion of politeness further strengthens my elucidation for the findings of my investigation. The final section of the chapter first looks into observations on women's politeness as well as prosodic features of their politeness in societies of America, New Zealand, Central American Indian Village (Tenajapa), and Japan. Chapter 5 finishes off with the discussion of the findings of my comparative investigation as it continues to explore the issue of voice pitch, politeness and gender. Discourse analyses of portions of my speech data provide pragmatic interpretations of voice pitch modulation here. They are supplemented in this chapter to demonstrate how context-dependent our voice pitch modulation could be as a support for my argument.

Politeness

Basic Understanding of Politeness

Lakoff's Rules of Politeness

Lakoff suggests that politeness is one of what she calls 'rules of pragmatic competence' (1973: 296). She defines politeness as something 'developed in societies in order to reduce friction in personal interaction' (Lakoff, 1975: 64). The concept of politeness constitutes the second rule of the two rules of pragmatic competence which are the rules of the cooperative principle established by Grice (1975). The first rules are rules of 'clarity.'

According to Lakoff (1975), the rules of politeness tell us why a particular act in a particular circumstance is polite or impolite. For her this predictability is the key feature of the rules. The three rules of politeness which Lakoff' (1973: 298) proposes are:

Rule 1. Formality: Remain aloof

Rule 2. Deference: Give options

Rule 3. Camaraderie: Be friendly

The purposes and examples of each rule of politeness which Lakoff (1973; 1975) suggested are as follows. Rule 1 creates a distance between speaker and addressee and a distance from the participants' topic. This rule effectively separates the subject from its emotional impact. The speaker's social status is usually superior to that of the addressee in this situation. Technical terms typically used by medical professionals with their patients such as 'copulation' and 'defecation' belong to this rule. Other examples of this rule are passive and impersonal expressions such as 'Dinner is served', and 'One feels awful about that.' Probably the most obvious example of Rule 1 is the use of titles plus last names in a formal situation (e.g., Ms. Skudra meeting her company CEO for the first time).

Rule 2 gives the addressee the option of deciding how to interpret what the speaker is saying. The superiority of the addressee over the speaker is often assumed in this kind of politeness. Hedges (e.g., John is sorta short) are often utilized to meet this rule of politeness. Rising question intonation used in a declarative statement (e.g., 'Dinner is ready?' uttered by a wife to her husband) and tag questioning are other examples. Euphemisms are also considered as Rule 2 type politeness.

Rule 3 makes the addressee feel that the speaker likes him and wants to be friendly with or interested in him. Use of colloquial language is one example of this rule. Nicknames, first names and last names alone (used in certain activities such as military or athletic training) would be additional examples of Rule 3 in action. Backslapping and jokes are included in the rule.

Brown and Levinson's Politeness Model

Brown and Levinson (1987: 1) begin their discussion on politeness by saying, 'like formal diplomatic protocol, (politeness) presupposes that potential for aggression as it seeks to disarm it, and makes possible communication between potentially aggressive parties.' Integral to their concept of politeness is an understanding of various strategies for inter-actional behavior based on two assumptions:

> Assumption 1: People are rational and thus capable of engaging in rational behavior to achieve satisfaction of certain wants (Brown and Levinson, 1987: 61).

> Assumption 2: They have two faces: a 'negative face' and a 'positive face.' Face is 'something that is emotionally invested, and that can be lost, maintained, or enhanced, and must be constantly attended to in interaction' (Brown and Levinson, 1987: 61).

Negative face represents the right to territory, freedom of action, and freedom from imposition. It has the want or desire that one's action not be restricted by others. Positive face symbolizes the positive self-image that people have and the want to be appreciated and approved of by others. Brown and Levinson also assume that certain kinds of actions may threaten both the addressee's and speaker's faces. They call these actions Face-Threatening Acts (FTA). The addressee's face can be threatened by speaker's behavior; or speaker's actions may entail threats to her own face. A request is a threat to one's negative face. It is an attempt to get someone else to do something that you wish done (meaning that the pursuit of the recipient's *own* desire is being imposed upon and thus her negative face is being intruded). Contradiction or expression of disagreement are examples of one's positive face being threatened. This means the speaker thinks that there is something wrong with the addressee's opinions or that the speaker is indifferent to the addressee's values.

The speaker's negative face can be threatened (e.g., by the possibility of rejection in asking a woman out for the first time). This occurs when the speaker is granting the addressee decision-making power and therefore forfeiting his own. Confessions, admissions of guilt, and apologies all threaten speaker's negative face. They suggest that the speaker has done something improper and that the addressee has the right to judge. On a nonverbal level, tripping and stumbling can be FTAs, suggesting that the actor is incapable. They reveal a certain incompetence in carrying out a fundamental action like walking.

When an FTA occurs, the rational person will normally look for ways of doing the act while minimizing the threat to face. Brown and Levinson propose five ways in which a person can deal with an FTA (Brown and Levinson, 1987: 69). If one does the FTA 'on record' (straightforwardly) with 'redressive actions', he can take advantage of either negative or positive politeness strategies.

Negative and positive politeness are based on negative and positive faces and involve ways of avoiding threats to one or the other. In negative politeness one's negative face want (to be free from imposition) is maintained and satisfied. Negative politeness is essentially avoidance-based and is characterized by self-effacement, formality, and restraint (Brown and Levinson, 1987: 129–30). By contrast, in *positive* politeness the speaker assumes the addressee shares the same cultural or moral values, with in-group rights, duties, and expectations of reciprocity (Brown and Levinson, 1987: 101–3).

Negative politeness strategies are employed in instances in which the FTA is clearly committed. Something else, however, is said or done to display concern for the other person's freedom of action and right not to be imposed upon. The most common of the ten strategies of negative politeness proposed by Brown and Levinson (1987: 131) is expressing reluctance to impose upon others. Examples are expressions such as ' I hate to ask you this, but would you do this for me?' and 'It would help me a lot if you would …' Other examples of this type of politeness strategy are 'question, hedge,' 'apologize,' 'impersonalize speaker and addressee,' 'be ambiguous', etc.

Strategies of positive politeness make the act less threatening by emphasizing that the speaker shares the addressee's interests and desires. Brown and Levinson suggest 15 examples of positive politeness strategies. The most universal of all the strategies is probably to avoid disagreement between speaker and addressee in the interest of finding common ground. Other positive politeness strategies mentioned by these authors include 'notice, attend to the addressee's interests, wants, needs, goods,' 'exaggerate (interest, approval, sympathy with addressee),' 'use of in-group identity markers,' 'seek agreement,' 'assert common ground,' 'joke,' and 'assume reciprocity.'

Ide's 'Discernment' Aspect of Politeness

Ide (1989), claiming that theories of linguistic politeness developed by Western linguists are not sufficient to account for to use of linguistic politeness in Japanese culture, proposes a supplementary concept, 'discernment.' She defines linguistic politeness as:

> the language usage associated with smooth communication, realized 1) through the speaker's use of intentional strategies to allow his/her message to be received favorably by the addressee, and 2) through the speaker's choice of expressions to confirm to the expressed and/or prescribed norms of speech appropriate to the contextual situation in individual speech communities. (Ide, 1989: 225)

She believes that there are two aspects of linguistic politeness. The first is *wakimae* (a Japanese term meaning 'discernment'). It is used to describe the practice of polite behavior according to social convention. Ide emphasizes the importance of the discernment aspect of linguistic politeness. The second aspect is referred to as 'the volitional' aspect of politeness (Hill *et al.*, 1986: 348). This allows the speaker a choice in expressing politeness from a wider range of possibilities, according to the speaker's intention.

By acting in conformity with the rules of discernment the speaker acknowledges his sense of place or role in a given situation. This is done according to his correct reading of his appropriate relative social distance from the addressee. The factors determining the distance between interlocutors are differences of social status, age, power, formality of participants and occasion, and topic (Ide, 1982). For the Japanese people, linguistic politeness is mainly a matter of conforming to social conventions. Linguistic forms such as pronouns, address terms, honorifics and other lexical items are used accordingly.

Thus, honorifics are not used to magnify the social standing of the addressee, but to acknowledge the status difference between speaker and referent (who is often the addressee). The user of honorifics assumes a status difference between the parties. In Ide's example below, the subject of the sentence, the professor, is given an honorific form in the predicate which is appropriate to her social standing. By using a referent honorific to mark the subject's deferential position, the speaker effectively displays her understanding of the referent's status as seen in the following example (Ide, 1989: 227).

(20) Sensei wa kore o **oyomi ni natta.**

referent honorific

'The professor read this.'

In another example, Ide indicates how a speaker accommodates to a formal situation where the speaker's status is lower than the addressee's. Here she uses both the morphologically encoded form of self-humbling (a humble honorific) and an addressee honorific (Ide, 1989: 229):

(21) Watasi ga   **mairi**   **masu.**

humble honoric addressee honorific

'I (will) go.'

Ide further mentions that the choice of forms available to speakers of honorific-using languages covers many parts of speech as copula, verbs, nouns, adjectives, and adverbs. The more elaborate the linguistic system of formality in a society, more important the part played by discernment. She concludes that languages with honorific systems have a strong preoccupation with discernment (Ide, 1989: 230–1). Ide posits that 'discernment' is not in conflict but in fact complementary with other theories of linguistic politeness. It also constitutes a part of their frameworks. 'Discernment' is partially accomplished by obeying the rules of 'formality' and 'deference' according to Lakoff's cosmology. It is a passive use of the strategy of 'giving deference' in Brown and Levinson's framework. However, if this strategy assumes the speaker's choice of using 'discernment,' then the concept is in conflict with their theoretical framework.

Politeness and Amae/Enryo for Japanese People

The concepts of *amae* (self-indulgence) and *enryo* (considerate restrain), which are peculiar to the Japanese, can be incorporated into two contrasting types of politeness. It follows that the action of *enryo* is exercised in Lakoff's Rule 1 (formality) or Brown and Levinson's negative politeness strategy ('Don't presume/assume'). The latter is subsumed under Brown and Levinson's negative politeness strategy 1 (Be conventionally indirect). *Enryo* can thus be exerted according to the convention of *wakimae*. *Enryo* distances the speaker from the addressee. It also serves to avoid presumptions being made about the addressee.

By contrast, *amae* can be explained to *sometimes* exist in Lakoff's Rule 3 (camaraderie) or be used for Brown and Levinson's positive politeness strategy 9 ('Presuppose concern for the addressee's wants'). One distinguishing element about the act of *amae* is that it can be either spontaneous or intentional in my opinion. My reasoning is that *amae* typically is more present in the human relationships in one's inner circle (*uchi*), in which acting self-indulgently is much more allowed compared with that in the outer circle (*soto*). Thus, the action of *amae* cannot always be performed according to rules of strategies of politeness. I do not believe that *amae* is fully dictated by the convention of *wakimae*, either. The feeling of *amae* is fundamentally a naturally occurring emotion with its essence originated from the self-indulgent feeling which infants experience with their mothers. Its act, therefore, cannot always be intentional or conventionalized. When visiting the US for the first time, Doi (1981: 11) could not accept his host's offer of ice cream even though he was hungry due to *enryo*. It dictated that he maintain formality or distance politeness in the face of meeting the host for the first time since he was socializing with someone who belonged to his outer (*soto*) circle. Doi felt that his relationship with his host was simply not one of *amae*, which would have allowed him to accept the host's first offer of ice cream. He could have accepted the offer from a close friend with whom he felt *amae* because his friend would belong to his inner (*uchi*) circle.

Prosodic Features of Politeness

The subject of prosodic features is a relatively minor issue in understanding the notion of politeness. Brown and Levinson observed certain prosodic features which constitute politeness strategies in the language of Tzeltal, a Central American Indian tribe, on which their study focused for a period of time.

In discussing prosodic hedges as a negative politeness strategy, Brown and Levinson observed a highly conventionalized use of high pitch or falsetto. This prosodic feature marks formal exchange, operating as a type of hedge on everything that is said in Tzeltal (the dialect spoken in the Tenejapa). The convention derive from children's extremely high voice pitch since 'the child has restricted rights to speak, restricted rights to demand the hearer's attention or response, and limited ability to speak with authority ' (Brown and Levinson, 1974: 10). Hence, when the speaker makes assertions with the 'ritualized falsetto', he 'makes minimal demands on the hearer, and pays him respect by avoiding any violation of his personal preserve' (Brown and Levinson, 1974: 10).

Use of this device, according to Brown and Levinson, insulates the speaker from responsibility for believing the truth of what s/he utters.

Brown and Levinson 's positive politeness strategy 2 ('Exaggerate') is seemingly done with exaggerated intonation, stress, and other features of prosody (1974: 104). Their English examples are:

(22) What a fanta'stic ga'rden you have!

(23) How absolutely extrao'rdinary!

Tamil is full of prosodic intensification in order to 'exaggerate interest, approval, sympathy with the addressee' as a deliberate strategy of positive politeness. One of Brown and Levinson's examples drawn from this language is (1974: 105):

(24) Ciile rompa aRakaana irukkiratu; on-oo Tiya nerattukku ituu ka Ttinaa, pramaatamaa irukku!

'That sari is very beautiful; for your coloring its' outstanding!'

Politeness, Expression of Emotion and Voice Pitch for Japanese People: My Findings

To elucidate the basic meaning of the two contrasting widths of pitch movement utilized by Japanese speakers it proves useful to consider the notions of *amae* and *enryo* as well as differences in politeness modes which the speakers adopt according to the convention of *wakimae*. I believe that all of these concepts are working together in their vacillating usage of voice pitch.

It is important to note that the changes in the use of pitch movements are closely related to the Japanese speakers' use of honorific forms. Honorifics express conventionalized politeness. Their use is dependent upon speakers' observations of the conventions of the society (*wakimae*) in which they are members (Ide, 1989). The social rules (*wakimae*) of politeness in Japanese dictate that speakers be polite according to (a) social position, power, and age of their interlocutors and (b) setting determined by their interlocutors and occasions (Ide, 1989: 366–77). The former rule approximately corresponds to Lakoff's politeness rule 2 (deference) while the latter roughly equates her rules 1 and 3 (formality/camaraderie). The use of honorifics in Japanese can be regarded as a negative politeness strategy to show social power/status differences and distance between the speakers. As demonstrated by Brown and Levinson, honorifics may in many cases be 'frozen outputs of face-oriented strategies' (Brown and Levinson, 1987: 279). Similarly, the use of plain forms (as opposed to honorific forms) can indicate that the speakers are employing positive politeness strategies to convey similarity to the address.

During the conversations which the Japanese informants hold with unfamiliar interlocutors, the politeness mode they use is a formal/deferential or negative politeness style due to *wakimae*. In this type of politeness, honorifics are used linguistically both to keep distance from and show deference toward the interlocutors. The pitch movements employed in this type of conversation are relatively narrow. I speculate that this is a result of the speakers' hesitancy to express feelings fully in a less comfortable social relationship which they hold with each other. A number of studies that have been conducted on emotion and voice pitch correlations as well as Scherer' 1986 review on these investigations indicate that emotions of less intensity, which include 'indifference,' are associated with decreases in mean F0 or suppression of pitch ranges. As Lebra (1976) pointed out, when *enryo* is necessary, Japanese people commonly restrain the expression of their feelings. Narrow pitch movements utilized in such a situation could be an indication of this suppression of their feelings. In Japanese society, speakers are perceived as being polite if they employ narrow pitch movements in public. This is the result of their suppressed use of wider pitch movements when dealing with unfamiliar people.

Let us look again at the utterance (3) in which a male Japanese informant reported an eccentric sushi restaurant. In expressing his amazement about the restaurant owner to an *unfamiliar* interlocutor, he maintains the expected style of speech for this situation by utilizing an addressee honorific form of copula, '*ndesu*.' The width of his pitch movements is relatively narrow throughout his utterance as even though he is recounting both amusing and amazing fact seen below:

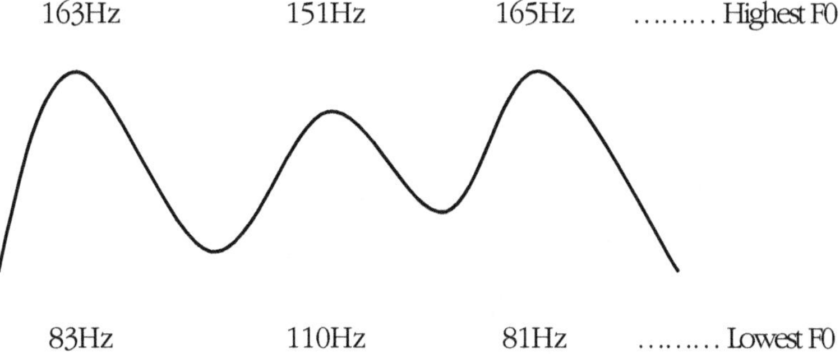

(18) Oonaa wa   itioo   nihonjin   rasii **ndesu**   yo.

   the owner   at least a Japanese seem   to be(I tell you)

Subject+Marker   Adv. Phrase Noun   Modality   Copula   Particle

Addressee Honorific

'The owner seems to be a Japanese person, at least (I tell you).'

When the same informant conversed with a familiar interlocutor, he dropped honorifics according to the *wakimae* rule and adopted wider pitch movements. The absence of honorifics appears to be an indication of the speakers' desires to be considered as equals and friends. Their use of widened pitch movements is a manifestation of this inclination to share their feelings more fully with the interlocutors. As a certain degree of *amae* is present in such a situation, speakers are able to express their 'selves' and expression of emotions was much more acceptable. This use of wider pitch movements, a display of emotional involvement, appears to be closely related to the politeness mode that people utilize in this situation: camaraderie or positive politeness. At least, such an outcome agrees with Brown's and Levinson's observations of exaggerated intonation patterns observed in the Tzeltal as expressions of positive politeness. All studies investigating emotion types and pitch characteristics consistently have reported the correlation between intense emotions labeled as 'elation' and increased pitch range width and variability of speech. One may reasonably speculate that these emotions result in wider pitch movements.

Now, let us contrast the above example with the nearly identical utterance made by the same male informant in the other situation. In this conversation, he describes the same restaurant proprietor to a *familiar* interlocutor using a plain form of copula '*da*.' The informant adopts considerably wider pitch movements than those employed in the previous situation.

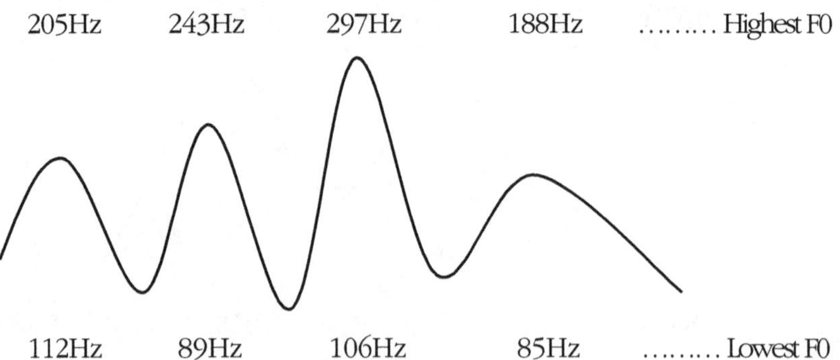

(19) Asoko no oonaa   nihonjin   mitai na   **nda**   kedo ne

　　 over there the owner a Japanese seem to be but (you know)

Location+Marker Subject Noun Phrase Modality Copula Connective Particle

Plain

'The owner over there seems to be a Japanese person, but… (you know).'

Politeness, Women and Voice Pitch

Politeness and American (Western) Women

Lakoff (1975) suggested that in traditional American society, women's politeness was covered by her Rule 1 (formality) and Rule 2 (deference) – establishing and reinforcing distance. Markers of camaraderie (Rule 3), backslapping, joke-telling, nicknaming, slang and so on were often avoided by females. She emphasized that women did not tell jokes for the purpose of creating a bonding relationship with the addressee. According to Lakoff, the reason we tell jokes is to become part of a (Rule 3 governed) bonding relationship, since joke-telling is a way of connecting tellers and hearers of jokes. Men typically use joke-telling as a device to create camaraderie. Thus, Lakoff argued that women avoid telling jokes from the fear that they may project a dangerously non-feminine image primarily because joke-telling was not part of women's conventional style.

The classic example of deference (Lakoff's Rule 2) used by women was the rule of tag question formation (Lakoff, 1975: 14). A tag question is halfway between a straightforward statement and a yes-no question. It is used when the speaker is making an assertion, but does not have enough confidence in its truth. Thus her statement is tentative. A good example provided by Lakoff is as follows (Lakoff, 1975: 16):

(25) The way prices are rising is horrendous, isn't it?

In this statement the speaker is expressing her opinion, but simultaneously seeking support from the addressee. Lakoff maintained that this sentence type allows speakers to avoid power conflicts with the addressee. It is a way of providing information without being pushy or domineering.

Some subsequent studies of tag-questions failed to verify Lakoff's claim about this phenomenon. It was found that depending on the context and intended function tag-questions appeared as frequently in male as female speech (Baumann, 1979; Dubois and Crouch, 1975).

Other more recent studies revealed that tag-questions do not always function as indicators of hesitancy or uncertainty as Lakoff originally suggested. Moreover, the two of these more recent and intricate studies of women's and men's use of linguistic features of tentativeness produced two opposing outcomes. The 1986 investigation by Preisler in England confirmed women's tendency to use tentative expressions (which included tag-questions) more frequently than men. The study further corroborated that women used those tentativeness indicators in single-gender as well as mixed-gender groups. Holmes collected data from women in New Zealand. By contrast, her results demonstrate that these expressions (including tag-questions) are *not* used by women as devices for expressing uncertainty. Rather, women here used the expressions in order to state their views with confidence, or as positive politeness strategies indicating solidarity with the addressee (Holmes, 1990: 202).

Lakoff (personal communication) notes that more recently American women's (and also men's) politeness has shifted more toward expressing and emphasizing camaraderie (Rule 3). Devices that are similar to male-intimacy-creating gestures, such as embraces and discussions of personal matters, are found among only all-female groups. She also mentions the use of words by women such as 'honey,' 'dear,' 'luv,' and so forth used between people who are not sexually or emotionally intimate. It is thus speculated that in contemporary American society tag-questions are used by American women more often as camaraderie politeness mechanisms (than *deferential* politeness devices) showing solidarity with the addressee.

Lakoff (1975: 56) notes that women have a wider variety of intonation patterns than men do. When women feel that they are not being listened to or taken seriously, they would use attention-catching voice patterns. She speculates that they use these extra intonational variations as a means of ensuring that their message is received and responded to (Lakoff, 1975: 57). Lakoff also points out that the phenomenon of rising intonation used in declarative answers to questions in the English language occurs predominantly in women's speech. This rising intonation, according to Lakoff, is used to seek confirmation even though the speaker may be the only person who knows the answer to the question. In the example (Lakoff, 1975: 17) which follows:

    (26) (a) A: when will dinner be ready?

         (b) B: Oh…around six o'clock …?

B's hesitant response requires A to state when a good time for dinner might be. Lakoff notes that the hesitancy of B's answer creates an intonation pattern which results in making women's speech sound more polite. This is a prosodic feature which would fulfill the requisites of her Rule 2 (Deference).

Edelsky's research conducted in 1979 did not support Lakoff's claim. In Edelsky's study (which utilized speakers of American English), the majority of informants, both female and male, used a falling intonation in reply to her questions. When asked to rate different intonation patterns, the informants perceived rising intonation as being more feminine. Lakoff never claimed that women always used rising intonation. I speculate that this impression is due to women's more frequent usage of rising intonation in certain contexts. However, there has not yet been any evident data found in support of that speculation.

Politeness and Japanese Women

Frequent uses of the deferential (honorific) prefix (*o-*) by Japanese women were observed in 1967 by Miller (289). However, the belief that Japanese women's speech is marked by the occurrence of formality/ deference or negative politeness was not confirmed until Ide's study.

Ide (1991) attempted to clarify the form of Japanese women's politeness and the reasons why politeness in Japanese women's speech is so notable. Based on the results of her questionnaires (to which 256 men and 271 women in their 40s and 50s responded) Ide found out that Japanese women typically chose more polite linguistic forms than men towards nine types of addressees (such as child, friend, neighbor and so forth) out of 12 (Ide, 1991: 67–8).

Ide also described other factors which contribute to women's politer speech. First, they avoid vulgar expressions and use of deprecatory suffixes, masculine final particles, and phonological reduction forms which carry derogatory connotations.

Since women are strongly discouraged from using vulgar expressions, they automatically sound as if they are persons with better demeanor. Demeanor defined as 'a display of desirable qualities,' makes women's speech naturally sound more polite.

Second, Ide speculated that women adopt 'beautification of honorifics and hypercorrect honorifics' (i.e., illegitimate uses of honorifics). Housewives' speech (as opposed to that of men and women in the workforce) is typically characterized by an abundance of such beautification honorifics. The honorific prefix (*o-*) is used for objects or actions of referents which are to be treated with deference. When it is used as a hypercorrection, however, it functions more as a way of giving the speaker a better image than actually placing special value on the objects and actions described, as the following example sentence illustrates (Ide, 1991: 74):

(27) Kono o-kane de o-yasai o kai masho.

'I'm going to buy vegetables with this money.'

In the following sentence deference is expressed for the speaker's mother in violation of the rule for the use of honorifics in Japanese. It is inappropriate to use referent honorifics with respect to one's mother, who is a member of one's in-group (Ide, 1991: 74):

(28) Haha ga **o**-kaeri-**ni-narimashita**.

referent honorific verb

'My mother came home.'

Here, too, the honorific is used to convey a better image of the speaker. Finally, both beautification of honorifics and hypercorrect honorifics are formal. This formality functions as a sign of good demeanor and thus makes these forms polite.

McGloin (1991) recognized two sentence-final particles (*wa* and *no*) typically used by women as signs of camaraderie (positive politeness). The sentence-final particle *wa* invests speech with an emotional resonance and thus engenders emotional rapport, empathy between speaker and addressee. She maintained that the rising intonation normally associated with the feminine *wa* should not be automatically associated with option-giving (negative politeness). Rather, it should be viewed as a sign of camaraderie (positive politeness). McGloin offers the following example (McGloin, 1991: 32):

(29) (a) A: *Samui ne.*   'It's cold, isn't it?'

(b) B: *Samui wa ne.*   'Really!'

Similarly, the sentence-final particle *no* is used more frequently by women due to its ability to create an atmosphere of shared knowledge, a conversational rapport between speaker and addressee. The example below expresses such an atmosphere of affinity (McGloin, 1991: 33).

(30) O-sashimi ga daisuki-na n(o) desu.

'I love sashimi, you know.'

Following Ide's and McGloin's studies on politeness of Japanese women's language in general, sociolinguists such as Smith (1992) commenced empirical researches on the speech of professional Japanese women holding authoritative positions, focusing on their politeness strategies. In 1994 and 1995, Sunaoshi conducted two case studies of the female shop managers at a family-owned camera/electronics shop. She maintained that the shop managers utilized politeness tactics which she calls 'collaboration (kyoowa)-oriented strategies.' They include frequent use of the sentence final particle '*ne*' which is a marker of empathy and rapport between managers and their subordinates. Sunaoshi indicates that these strategies allow the female managers to 'show their attentiveness and create rapport and initiate a comfortable rhythm for conversation' for the effective issuing of directives (Sunaoshi, 1994: 687). Moreover, Furo (1996) examined naturally occurring interactions of female teachers in the classroom setting while managing to resolve their challenges. She found that female teachers routinely adopted the sentence-final particle '*ne*' as one of positive politeness strategies to promote solidarity in achieving illocutionary force.

More recently, Takano (2005) revealed the importance of positive politeness strategies which professional Japanese women in leadership positions use in communicating powerfully. He states that positive politeness is used by these women as 'rapport builders for symmetrical interpersonal relationships and voluntary collaboration' (Takano, 2005: 633). Takano obtained the result from large-scale on-site observations of authentic workplace interactions. A grand total of 752 directive speech acts and exchanges directives from nine female subjects and 122 directives from eight male subjects, both in positions of authority) were elicited.

He analyzed surface morphosyntactic structures of the directives by revising the classification system of nine directive types[1] originally formulated by Blum-Kulka *et al.*'s (1989b: 18). He noted that both positive and negative politeness strategies coexist in their strategic language use in the following manner (Takano, 2005: 656). In highly face-threatening situations, these women resorted to style shifting, in which they negotiate their in-group/out-group (uchi/soto) memberships. Using downward shifts from formal style to casual style created in-group solidarity. By contrast, in using upward shifts from casual style to formal style, these women deliberately detach themselves from in-group camaraderie that has just been established in the preceding context. The following excerpt, derived from a long delivery of a 45-year-old supervisor at a foreign language:

> school admonishing the subordinates who are in a faculty meeting
> to clean up teaching materials, demonstrates the foregoing.
> (Takano, 2005: 655)

(31) … De ichiban … komatta no wa ne, risuningu tasuku no ano orijinaru ga <u>nakunatchatteru</u>.

Casual style

'And most troublesome is that the originals (of the materials) for the listening tasks *are gone.*'

(32) Dakara ano, So, um, orijinaru wa, moo nani ga attemo <u>modoshite kudasai</u> ne.

Formal style

'The originals, *please return* them no matter what happens.'

According to Takano, these professional women are aware that they succeeded in inducing favorable responses or support from the subordinates by reducing social distance from them by the use of positive politeness strategies as solidarity markers. When using negative politeness strategies as displays of deference and respect, these women may appear as if they are underplaying their status. However, negative politeness can help enhance the speaker's prestige and power since this type of politeness simultaneously emphasizes the social distance from the addressees. Takano (2005: 658) speculates that these professional women recognize this twist of using negative politeness.

The 1995 *New York Times* article introduced in Chapter 1 is also relevant here. Female elevator operators employed at department stores in Japan have been known to utilize conspicuously high-pitched voices in greeting customers. The unnaturally high-pitched voice which these women use is artificially produced. This is intentionally done because high-pitched voice serves as politeness which store employees display towards their customers. It is one of the approaches which women take in order to sound tentative and thus polite, much like the way American women sometimes use tag-questions or make statements with rising intonation. Female employees in service industries in general in this society appear to undergo a similar process in order to speak with clients in this desirable high-pitched voice. It is the 'conventionalized falsetto' which Brown and Levinson observed among Tenejapan people as a negative politeness device due to the speakers' 'limited ability to speak with authority' (Brown and Levinson, 1974: 10).

Loveday's (1981) cross-cultural study of voice pitch also reports that only his Japanese female informants utilized similarly conspicuous high-pitched voices in greetings such as 'hello' and 'thank you' in a constructed dialogue. In addition, Ohara's (1999) study indicates that only the female bilingual subjects (both Japanese and Americans) adopt higher average pitch when speaking in Japanese than in English. Ohara's investigation involved having her subjects request a professor for his/her book by leaving a telephone message. Again, I believe that high-pitched voice employed by the female informants in the aforementioned studies is the 'conventionalized use of falsetto,' which Brown and Levinson detected in 1974. According to them, through the use of this 'ritualized falsetto' the speaker reduces the directness of any demands toward the addressee to a minimum, and is able to avoid violating his/her personal territory (Brown and Levinson, 1974: 10).

Thus, Brown's observations regarding Tenejapan women's prosodic features of politeness shed an interesting light on the on-going discussion. Women in the Tenejapan community characteristically speak in a high pitch falsetto voice in the presence of men (Brown, 1980). Brown interprets this prosodic characteristic as being highly deferential and self-effacing (avoidance-type negative politeness). She claims that a function of the falsetto is to liberate the speaker from being responsible for her utterance. In using a high pitch voice Tenejapan women therefore keep communication with men conflict-free.

Furthermore, in Tzeltal the exaggeration in positive politeness with its emphasized prosodic features is evidently quite conspicuous. Tenejapan women, particularly, sounds like actors in a play emphasizing on displays of camaraderie. In this language, speech eliciting the addressee's sympathy uses heightened pitch variations, emphatic stress, rhythmicity, and exaggerated intonation contours. A woman describing the disreputable appearance of her drunken husband to a church crowd said (with these emphasized prosodic features marked with apostrophes) as follows (Brown and Levinson 1987: 105–6):

> (33) He lo'oked as i'f he was sti'll dru'nk; he looked
> incre'dibly di'rty, re'ally u'nco'mbed ha'ir, re'ally
> cro'oked clo'thes, re'ally his be'lt ha'lf-fi'ed!

Gender, Voice Pitch and Politeness: My Findings

Women

Most Japanese female informants in my investigations seem to exaggerate pitch movements made at highest frequencies when conversing with familiar interlocutors. Seemingly, they are trying to reach their highest possible pitch level. There were occasions when some female Japanese informants used pitch in excess of 500 Hz, the level which makes a voice sound like a squeak. This extremely high pitch constituted those short pitch movements made at high frequencies.

In Japan, in the 1990s it was reported that women (both young and middle-aged) began using less feminine linguistic styles (Okamoto and Sato, 1992; Y. Matsumoto, 1999b). Takekuro (2004), however, reported that her female informants utilized less feminine linguistic forms until they finished college although they resumed the use of more feminine linguistic styles upon the entry into new social roles.

As far as paralinguistic style is concerned, however, Japanese women may continue utilizing a high-pitched voice as a reflection of the persistent societal expectation to project a feminine image. In my data which was obtained from both college students and interns volunteering in a non-profit organization, there were incidences of extremely high pitch. This follows from the fact that appearing feminine is still important in this society.

Van Bezooijen's (1996) study (which focused on Japanese and Dutch women's pitch) revealed that Japanese listeners (both men and women) perceived Japanese women's medium and high pitch as more appealing than Dutch listeners (both men and women) did. Moreover, the surveys conducted in 2000 on gender desirability rating by psychologists found that Japanese men continuously expect women to possess feminine personality traits (Sugihara and Katsurada). It is my opinion that Japanese women still prefer being perceived as feminine and (consequently) attractive by continuing to use high pitch.

It is worth returning to the *New York Times* article (by Kristof) discussion of Japanese women's desire to speak with a lower or more natural voice pitch. A teenage girl in Tokyo interviewed in this article confessed her annoyance by other Japanese girls speaking in very high voices. She also expressed her frustration she felt when her mother asked her to raise her naturally low voice. The article includes a comment by a bilingual reporter at *Asahi* newspaper on Japanese men's attraction toward high voices and girlish behaviors, which some Japanese women emulate. A lower voice apparently sounds too forceful and masculine to the ear of Japanese men. The reporter, like other bilingual women such as those who participated in Ohara's studies, speaks in a higher pitched voice in Japanese and lowers it when speaking English.

However, Kasuya came to the reverse conclusion in the 1996 *Daily Yomiuri* article (by Muranaka), finding a trend for female newscasters to use a lower pitch. This researcher feels that an unnaturally articulated low voice by female speakers sounds unpleasant due to the unsuited vocal apparatus and artificial use of vocal cords. In his opinion, as long as the voice pitch does not exceed 250 Hz, it is not perceived as too high pitched. In addition, The *Daily Yomiuri* article also includes a comment by one of the newscasters stating that she does feel strain in her vocal cords when trying to lower her voice pitch and that her voice naturally rises when her health condition is not at its best. In my opinion, this is evidence showing that Japanese women feel ambivalent toward their speaking voice pitch. Furthermore, as shown in Chapter 3, Japanese female informants' overall pitch range is actually similar to that of their American counterparts when they are conversing with *unfamiliar* interlocutors (see Figures 3.5 and 3.7). Their average lowest and highest pitch levels expressed in Hertz are nearly identical to those of American counterparts (see Figure 3.9). It is in fact the case that Japanese female voice encompasses a wide spectrum of pitches and varies considerably depending on what the societal and situational expectations dictates them.

By contradistinction, female voice seems to have been generally lowering in American society. Interestingly, I observed not only American female informants' lower average highest pitch levels (than Japanese female informants), but also the more frequent use of creaky voice by American as compared to Japanese women (Yuasa, 2003; 2006; 2007). Creaky voice refers to 'a vocal effect produced by a very slow vibration of only one end of the vocal cords' (Crystal, 1997: 98). Thus, the creaky voice generates very low pitch which is normally below an individual's natural voice pitch range; because of the abnormal nature of its phonation, whenever detected, creaky voices were eliminated from my analyses. I speculate that this low-pitched creaky voice in reality further contributes to the general image of American women as not only being low-pitched but also wide-pitched.

American women may intuitively recognize that individual and professional success depends on assimilation within the dominant group (i.e., male). Consequently they may resort to altering their behavior by adopting that group's values (Tajfel, 1982). A lowering of overall pitch by consciously suppressing the use of high pitch is one approach which women take in order to accomplish this assimilation (Coates, 1986: 10). In Chapter 1, I demonstrated how women's high-pitched voice is generally disfavored in American society. The negative and admonishing attitude towards women's high voices seen in popular novels and etiquette handbooks as well as scholars' remarks may have in fact contributed to this phenomenon of lowering American women's voice pitch.

Therefore, in 1965, comments were also made on American women's desire to speak with low-pitched voices by Austin, Luchsinger, and Arnold. Austin recalled that 50 years prior to his comment all ladies had spoken with high pitched voices. Moreover, Linke's (1973) investigation suggested that American women might possibly be utilizing pitch levels that are lower than desirable for the most effective usage of their voices in speech. Narrower pitch ranges with lower baselines (than Japanese women) employed when conversing with familiar interlocutors may, thus, be the result of American women's unconscious strategies to conform to dominant male characteristics.

'Swoopy' or 'Squeaky' Image of Women's Voice Characteristics

With regard to the median pitch movement widths employed by men and women expressed in what is considered the most appropriate frequency scale (the ERB), they did not show conspicuously different values. This finding was consistent across the languages of Japanese and American English. This means that the overall width of women's pitch ranges is not perceived by the human ear as being as wide as one would normally assume. Nevertheless, a commonly held stereotype of American women's speech is 'swoopy' and that of Japanese women 'squeaky.'

The length of vocal cords is the major physical factor determining the fundamental frequency of an individual's voice (Titze, 1989). Anatomically, women tend to have shorter vocal cords than men do. This means that it is easier for women to produce sounds with higher frequencies than it is for men. Pitch movements reaching high frequencies constitute considerably wide overall pitch ranges. The same consequence, however, cannot be accomplished by lowering the baseline of our pitch since there is a limit as to how far the baseline can be lowered. Pitch excursions made at high frequencies by Japanese women can create narrow or short pitch ranges if the baseline of that pitch range is raised. Thus, American women may occasionally utilize much wider pitch movements than their male counterparts. In the case of Japanese women, they may sporadically make small pitch movements at high frequencies. These extremely large pitch movements or short pitch movements produced at high frequencies typically occurred only a few times every minute.

Pitch range researchers have excluded these extreme values of pitch from the statistics. Their reasoning here is that the extreme pitch values *may* create a deceptive impression of overall pitch of an individual. Nevertheless, it may be the case that people choose to describe women's speech characteristics based mainly on such infrequent features as extremely wide pitch movements or movements occurring within the higher end of women's pitch register. Or, they may not pay close attention to detailed information about women's communication style and speculate about it.

Ruscher and Fiske (1990) noted that people attend more to stereotype-consistent information than they do to information that is inconsistent with stereotypes. Thus, people in general invoke stereotypes even when the individual being discussed does not display stereotypical behavior (Ruscher and Hammer, 1994). Moreover, people present information congruous with stereotypes in more abstract and general terms with respect to information which is incongruous with such stereotypes (Maass, Salvi, Arcuri, and Semin, 1989). For instance, 'people might describe a woman generally as "emotional" but a man more concretely as "being upset"' (cited in Carli and Bukatko, 2000: 295). It is the case that people in general may not pay close attention to detailed information about women's communication style and make inferences in making judgments about it.

I contend that Japanese and American people are inclined to pay attention to those few extreme pitch movements (made by American women) or movements occurring at the higher end of women's registers (made by Japanese women) in depicting women's speech style. The former type of expression is characterized as 'swoopy,' the latter as 'squeaky.' Each contributes to stereotypical assessments of women's speech in general terms. People may thus inaccurately believe that women's speech style is *emphatic* based on such salient prosodic features.

Women's Wide Pitch Movements and Those made at High Pitch Levels as Means of Camaraderie/positive Politeness

Women's occasional usage of wide or high-pitched voice characteristics can be construed in more neutral terms of camaraderie/positive politeness. Moreover, these pitch characteristics can also be interpreted with regard to women's 'cooperative conversation styles' in which women mutually support each other's viewpoints in an effort to generate a collaborative atmosphere of interaction.

Lakoff observed that American women (as well as men) recently have begun exhibiting and stressing camaraderie more so than previously. While men regularly tell jokes, slap each other's backs, and use slang to demonstrate their camaraderie, women typically display behaviors such as embraces and communication of personal issues to accomplish the same objective. Moreover, Lakoff adds that American women (as opposed to men) use words such as 'honey,' 'dear,' 'luv,' and so on toward people who are not sexually or emotionally intimate. It is noteworthy that men who might make the same word choices do so in a manner usually laden with sexual connotation.

There is also a considerable body of research suggesting that in a variety of situations American women are supportive and cooperative conversationalists (e.g., Thorne *et al.*, 1983). They have also been specifically described as 'interactively facilitative and positive politeness-oriented participants' (Holmes 1993: 92). For example, one researcher found that in informal committee meetings, women participated more actively when the 'floor' of talk encouraged more casual and collaborative atmosphere, which also gave rise to a simultaneous interaction between speakers (Edelsky, 1981: 416).

I emphasize that women's occasional usage of wide or high-pitched voice characteristics is simply a reflection of their camaraderie/positive politeness style. I propose that women intermittently adopt such paralinguistic features as a way of 'entering into a bonding relationship with each other.' For American women, their wide pitch movements are equivalent to physical embraces and intimate words (such as 'dear' and 'honey'). In the following excerpts, American female informants entertain each other regarding chicken feet served at a Chinese restaurant which they dined, using ample of wide pitch movements. The pitch movements of intonation groups are expressed in E values in the ERB scale.

(34) (a) AF1: So, did you eat/the chicken feet?

             2.4   2

(b) AF2: Chicken feet! I'm sure it tastes/fine, but …

             2.7   2.9   0.6

It was really cracking me up to watch/other people, you

             2.7   2.7

know.

(c) They kind of look like you nibble your own finger.

                     2.7

(35) (a) AF2: Totally, you ate some chicken feet.

                     4.3

(b) AF1: I did.

     2.3

Japanese women neither embrace nor exchange such intimate words with each other in the casual way that American women do since their cultural norms classify those behaviors as sexually intimate (and thus unacceptable). Thus, Japanese women are more likely to resort to other means of demonstrating their camaraderie such as modulating their pitch. Pitch movements produced at high pitch levels are excellent vehicles for establishing such comradeship. Conspicuousness of these prosodic features creates a sense of excitement about the subject. In the following two discourses gleaned from my speech data, Japanese female informants (JF1, JF2, and JF3) reached significantly high pitch levels. JF1 and JF2 appear to have done this in educing each other's agreement and JF3 in creating a sense of excitement. The highest pitch levels of intonation groups are indicated in terms of Hertz values.

(36) (a) JF2: Uuun, datte moo/Ai Hausu no (mazui) gohan, nare tyatta!

    250   410

 '... I got used to the (bad) food at the I-House!'

(b) JF1: Areyori/hidoi no wa/nai daroo mitai na.

   413   313   214

 'It seems as if nothing is worth than that.'

(37) (a) JF4: Nanka ne. Uni ga ne, tyoo nokkatte ru.

 'I heard. (There is) Sushi with lots of sea urchin roe over (the rice).'

(b) JF3: *Aaa, Tabetai*!

   552

 'Wow, I wanna eat!'

(c) JF4: Moo, suggoi! Sano-san ga itte te sa.

 'It's amazing, Mr Sano said.'

(d) JF3: *Doko, doko?*

   308

 'Where, where is it?'

(e) JF4: *Kikoo yo.*

 'Let's ask him.'

(f) JF3: San Huransisuko kana?

   391

 'I wonder if it's in San Francisco.'

(g) JF4: Un. Atti no hoo.

'Yeah, it's over there.'

(h) JF3: San Huransisuko! Ippai/atta mon ne.

536   552   446

'San Francisco! There were lots (of Japanese restaurants there) I remember.'

I observed the similar tendency in the data in which female informants conversed with familiar male interlocutors. In the discourse below, a Japanese female informant (JF7) reached noticeably high pitch levels in conversing with a male informant. She seems to have utilized such high pitches in eliciting her male addressee's (JM6) agreement.

(38) (a) JM6: ... ano hen no tabete kotti kuru to,

'If you come here after eating (Mexican food) over there

kanari jadoo da to omoo.

I think (Mexican food here) is pretty bad.'

(b) JF7: Ah, honto ni! Mekisiko to/ka demo...

512   480   /   296

'Oh, really! Even Mexican food ...'

Honba wa/ wakarai kedo,

424   /   349

'I don't know what the authentic one tastes like, but

watashi ni totte wa /saikoo da ne.

356   /   320

Mexican food here is great for me.'

(c) JM6: Naruhodo, naruhodo.

'I see, I see.'

Emphasizing such feelings as interests, approval, and sympathy toward the addressee is important for creating a feeling of camaraderie (Brown and Levinson, 1987). It is my premise that both Japanese and American women, therefore, utilize voice pitch characteristics in order to exaggerate such feelings. Their use of these paralinguistic features, in turn, also contributes to creating a collaborative and supportive atmosphere of conversation, which is a positive alternative to the dominating and competitive mode of interaction typically used by men.

Men

Seward (1968: 111) observed Japanese men's effort to emphasize the masculinity of their speech through their use of a deep-voiced, rough style of speaking. This representation was noted in Loveday's (1981) data in which he detailed his male Japanese informants' use of lower and flatter pitch ranges compared to Englishmen's pitch ranges. The results derived from Loveday's male Japanese informants were similar to the outcome obtained from my male Japanese informants (during the conversations with an unfamiliar interlocutor) in the previous experiment. Japanese men in *both* studies employed relatively flat and narrow pitch ranges with lower base mean F0 than their Western counterparts.

However, when my male informants interacted with *familiar* interlocutors, their pitch ranges became considerably wider. Their behavioral orientation in a social setting changed depending on whether they operated in the inner or outer circle. That is, they chose honorifics when speaking to people located in their 'outer circle.' In contradistinction, they switched to *non*-honorific plain forms when conversing with people within their 'inner circle.' Social protocol gave rise to emphasizing characteristics of two distinctive politeness styles according to these two contrasting relationships ('inner and outer'). In so doing, the Japanese are able to display their social competence as mature members of the society.

Because of the existence of these contrasting perspectives, the Japanese male informants' maximal pitch ranges were nearly twice as wide as those of American males. These extreme pitch movements were also as wide as those of their female counterparts in terms of the E-values of the ERB-scale. They utilized emphatically wider pitch ranges in demonstrating inner-oriented characteristics (and camaraderie/positive politeness) to familiar interlocutors. It is precisely within this inner circle that Japanese are expected to behave freely without concern for propriety. This Japanese male informants' tendency evidenced how capable male speakers are of widening their pitch ranges considerably if a compelling socio-cultural reason (such as creating camaraderie) convinces them to do so.

In comparison, American male informants did not utilize as wide a voice pitch movement as any other groups in my study. Possibly, the American males might not have chosen to express camaraderie in terms of prosodic means as much due to their disinclination to show camaraderie/positive politeness. In the 1980s American men's inexpressiveness was debated by male researchers in several fields (Sattel, 1983; Balswick, 1988; Connel, 1995). They generally brought forth the idea of men's suffering the constraints of their own prohibitive gender roles. It was theorized that men, too, were victimized by society's role expectations. It was proposed that men were unable to express their emotions with the same clarity as women due to the pressure of a patriarchal society demanding that they appear rational and unemotional (Seidler, 1989: 123–42). American males' narrower pitch ranges, detected in my study, and their lower average F0 compared to European (Polish) males (reported in 1972 by Majewski, Hollien and Zalewski), might, in fact, reflect these researchers' viewpoints. The idea here is presumably that if men could only free themselves from such constraints, they would be more satisfied and fulfilled human beings. I speculate that this inexpressiveness characterizing American men may be reflected in their voice pitch modulation.

In my speech data I observed an occasion where American male informants appear to have utilized relatively wide pitch movements as positive politeness devices. They sounded as if they were attempting to bond through the use of emphatic intonation. In the following excerpt acquired from my speech data, two male American informants (AM5 and AM6) employed considerably wide voice pitch excursions in eliciting the addressee's sympathy or agreement. Note that when the pitch movements of intonation groups are expressed in values on the ERB scale, they are nearly as wide as those used during the interactions between their female counterparts in the aforementioned discourse examples.

(39) (a) AM5: (Explaining a type of sushi called '*inari*') It's a little envelope thing, a kind of brownish color. They put that around rice and then on top they put the crab. It's, oh god, so good.

(b) AM6: I really don't like crab. I only/ had once actually.

　　　　3.6　　　　　　　　　2.4　　　　　2

(c) Other two stupid friends wanted to go there.

　　　　　0.9

(d) Stupid. It wasn't all that good. I didn't like crab.

　　　2.5　　　　　　　　　2.9　　　　　2

(e) AM5: Really!

(40) (a) AM6: I like Carols Junior. I like their, what is it,
            their chicken sandwich. Chicken sandwich is pretty much
            the only thing you can count on, but it's like ...
      (b) AM5: Say, Say, it's like, people like/Carlos Junior. It's
                 2.7 0.8   1.6   1.8
            usually/ chicken sandwich!
                 0.8   3.1

   (c) AM6: Really!

In sum, I emphasize that American male speakers are indeed both
able and willing to significantly widen their overall voice pitch ranges if
a socio-cultural norm of expressing camaraderie allows them to do so.

Notes

1. In descending order of forcefulness/directness, Takano's revised system
    consists of four types of acts with respective directive statements (Takano,
    2005: 640):
    1) Direct Act I
        (i)   Mood derivable ('Do X.')
        (ii)   Performatives ('I am asking you to do X.')
        (iii) Hedged performatives ('I would like to ask you to do X.')
        (iv)   Want statements ('I want you to do X.')
    2) Direct Act II
        (v)   Locution derivable ('You'll have to do X.')
    3) Conventionally Indirect Act
        (vi)   Suggestory formulae ('How about doing X?')
        (vii) Query preparatory ('Could you do X?')
    4) Non-conventionally Indirect Act
        (viii) Hints.

6 Conclusion: Interpreting Variations Of Voice Pitch Modulation Across Culture And Gender

My findings in this book, I believe, demonstrate the importance of scrutinizing the complexity of voice pitch modulation which men and women across cultures employ in conversational speech. Impressionistic observations of men's and women's voice pitch characteristics of everyday speech offer merely subjective views of the perception of their voice pitch attributes. They only function to preserve stereotypical beliefs about men's and women's voice pitch although admittedly, they simultaneously inform us about our attitudes toward certain voice pitch characteristics. The outcome of acoustic analyses utilizing speech data not drawn from conversational speech (i.e., vowel sounds uttered and passages or constructed dialogues read by informants as well as impromptu speech and simulated task-completion) provide limited information about men's and women's voice pitches. They do not reveal how voice pitch fluctuations convey socio-cultural meanings in a broad sense at the same time with depth. By contrast in this study I have undertaken a cross-cultural comparison which derives its speech data from spontaneously generated conversations. Such an approach provides evidence of how culture and universal human behaviors as well as gender intersect with each other. I have also sought to show how a consideration of emotion and politeness leads to a better understanding of men's and women's voice pitch fluctuations. Attention to these universal human behaviors allow for a meaningful comparing between the speech obtained from two such different cultures as Japan and America.

I first invoked the cultural aspect of pitch movement characteristics in elucidating their roles. I suggested that the pitch range modulation displayed by Japanese informants in two types of conversations was closely linked to types of politeness which the informants adopted in interacting with each other. I also indicated that the differences in the degree of the informants' emotional involvement and expressions reflected in the differing pitch range widths plays an important role in determining the relationship between pitch range modulation and politeness. The phenomenon was strongly associated with the Japanese cultural concepts of *amae* and *enryo*, which are also closely connected to the displays of emotion and politeness. I proposed the importance of integrating the concept of emotion into that of politeness in making intelligible the socio-cultural roles of voice pitch movement characteristics.

I then addressed gender phenomena of voice pitch movements. The results of my analyses indicated that when the most appropriate frequency scale for speech perception (the ERB-scale) was used, the difference between male and female pitch movements across cultures was not as large as one would expect as far as median values are concerned. I, however, found that pitch characteristics, which may have contributed to the impressionistic image of women's speech, differ in Japanese and American cultures. I suggested that the salience of these differing voice pitch characteristics had become stereotypically associated with women's speech sounding arguably 'swoopy' or 'squeaky.' I then further proposed that it is more sensible to regard women's wide-pitched or high-pitched voice characteristics (which appear to have contributed to a gender-stereotyped image of women) as manifestations of another socio-cultural behavior of politeness (i.e., camaraderie/positive politeness). Furthermore, I emphasized that Japanese men's use of wide pitch movements found during conversations with familiar interlocutors displayed the extent to which male speakers are able to enlarge pitch ranges *if* they are truly motivated to do so.

Perhaps the most important contribution which this volume makes, therefore, is demonstrating how men's and women's voice pitch can be interpreted in terms of an interaction between socio-cultural behavioral norms (other than gender) and gender expectations. I have sought to show how voice pitch, an unconscious linguistic property, is indeed capable of revealing this kind of intersection of various socio-cultural aspects of human behavior. However, without using the innovative methodologies (such as interdisciplinary and comparative perspectives which my investigation adopted), I do not believe that we are able to genuinely understand the complexities of human behaviors (which include linguistic and paralinguistic behaviors). Such a multi-faceted approach to the investigation of intricate human behaviors constitutes an obligatory aspect of any future research.

Finally, high and low pitch should not elicit negative value judgments since they are merely levels of sound on a relative auditory scale.

An individual should be able to use a pitch range that is physically natural and comfortable as well as appropriate for the specific social situations. People should not have to feel that their pitch range needs to be modified. Numerical results derived from culture- and gender-related speech data, such as this volume's investigation, may not be able to eliminate existing stereotypes. But it may prompt people to reconsider and reconstitute their ways of looking at the world. Invoking an analogy in music, we see that all singers (soprano, alto, tenor, and baritone) are valuable. It is the combination of *all* the voice ranges which make it possible for a choir to create beautifully orchestrated harmony.

References

Abe, I. (1955) Intonational patterns of English and Japanese. *Word* 11(3): 386–98. Reprint (1972) In D. Bolinger (ed.) *Intonation: Selected Readings* 337–47. Harmondsworth: Penguin Books Ltd.

Alcott, L. M. (1867) *Little Women*. V. Alderson (ed.) (Oxford World's Classics). Oxford: New York: Oxford University Press (UK).

Armstrong, L. E. and Ward, I. S. (1926) *Handbook of English Intonation*. Leipzig: Teubner.

Austin, W. M. (1965) Some social aspects of paralanguage. *Canadian Journal of Linguistics* 11: 31–9.

Bachnik, J. M., Charles J. and Quinn, Jr. (1994) *Situated Meaning: Inside and Outside in Japanese Self, Society, and Language*. Princeton, NJ: Princeton University Press.

Balswick, J. (1988) *The Inexpressive Male*. Lexington, MA: Lexington Books.

Banse, R. and Scherer, K. R. (1996a) Acoustic profiles in vocal emotion expression. *Journal of Personality and Social Psychology* 70(3): 614–36.

Bard, P. (1934) On emotional expression after decortication with some remarks on certain theoretical views. *Psych. Reviews* 41: 309–29.

Baumann, M. (1976) Two features of women's speech. In B. L. Dubois and I. Crouch (eds) *Proceedings of the Conference on the Sociology of the Language of American women*. San Antonio, TX: Trinity University.

Beier, E. G. and Zautra, A. J. (1972) Identification of vocal communication of emotions across cultures. *Journal of Consulting and Clinical Psychology* 39: 166.

Birdwhistell, R. L. (1970) *Kinesics and Context*. Philadelphia, PA: University of Pennsylvania Press.

Blum-Kulka, S., House, J., Kasper, G. (1989b) Investigating cross-cultural pragmatics: an introductory overview. In S. Blum-Kulka, J. House and G. Kasper (eds) *Cross-cultural Pragmatics: Requests and Apologies (Advances in Discourse Processes 31)* 1–34. Norwood, NJ: Ablex.

Bolinger, D. L. (1986) *Intonation and its Parts: Melody in Spoken English*. Stanford, CA: Stanford University Press.

Bolinger, D. L. (1989) *Intonation and its Uses: Melody in Grammar and Discourse*. London: Edward Arnold.

Brazil, D. (1981) The place of intonation in a discourse model. In M. Coulthard and M. Montgomery (eds) *Studies in Discourse Analysis* 146–157. London: Routledge & Kegan Paul.

Brazil, D., Coulthard, M., and Johns, C. (1980). *Discourse Intonation and Language Teaching.* London: Longman.

Brown, P. (1980) How and why are women more polite: some evidence from a Mayan community. In S. McConnell-Ginet, R. Borker, N. Furman (eds) *Women and Language in Literature and Society.* New York: Praeger Publishers.

Brown, P. and Levinson, S. (1987) *Politeness: Some Universals in Language Usage. Studies in Interactional Sociolinguistis 4.* Cambridge: Cambridge University Press.

Campbell, N. and Erickson, D. (2004) What do people hear? A study of the perception of non-verbal affective information in conversational speech. *The Journal of the Phonetic Society of Japan* 8 (1): 9–26.

Cannon, W. B. (1927) The James-Lange theory of emotion: A critical examination and an alternative theory. *American Journal of Psychology* 39: 106–24.

Carli L. L. and Bukatcko, D. (2000) Gender, communication, and social influence: a developmental perspective. In T. Eckes and H. M. Trautner (eds) *The Developmental Social Psychology of Gender* 295–331. Mahwah, NJ: Lawrence Erlbaum Associates, Publishers.

Catford, J. C. (1977) *Fundamental Problems in Phonetics.* Bloomington, IN: Indiana University Press.

Clark, A. J. R. (1999) Using prosodic structure to improve pitch range variation in text to speech synthesis. *The Proceedings of the 14th International Congress of Phonetic Sciences* 69–72.

Couper-Kuhlen, E. and Selting, M. (1996) Towards an interactional perspective on prosody and prosodic perspective on interaction. In E. Couper-Kuhlen and M. Selting (eds) *Prosody in Conversation (Studies in Interactional Sociolinguics 12)* 11–56. Cambridge: Cambridge University Press.

Coates, J. (1986) *Women, Men, and Language.* London: Longman.

Connel, R.W. (1995) *Masculinities.* Oxford: Polity Press.

Cowan, M. (1936) Pitch and intensity characteristics of stage speech. *Archives of Speech* 1(Supplement): 1–92.

Crawford, J., Kippax, S., Onyx, J., Gault, U., and Benton, P. (1992) *Emotion and Gender: Constructing Meaning from Memory.* London: Sage.

Cruttenden, A. (1986) *Intonation.* Cambridge: Cambridge University Press.

Crystal, D. (1969) *Prosodic Systems and Intonation in English.* Cambridge: Cambridge University Press.

Crystal, D. (1971) Prosodic and paralinguistic correlates of social categories. In E. Ardener (ed.) *Social Anthropology and Language.* London: Tavistock.

Crystal, D. (1997) *A Dictionary of Linguistics and Phonetics.* Oxford: Blackwell Publishers.

Darwin, C. (1871) Secondary sexual characters of mammals. *Descent of Man.* London: J. Murray. Chap. XVIII: Part II.

Darwin, C. R. (1872) *The Expression of the Emotions in Man and Animals.* London: John Murray

De Pinto, O. and Hollien, H. (1982) Speaking fundamental frequency characteristics of Australian women: then and now. *Journal of Phonetics* 10: 367–75.

Doi, T. (1981) *The Anatomy of Dependence*. Tokyo: Kodansha International.

Dubois, B. L. and Crouch, I. (1975) The question of tag questions in women's speech: they don't really use more of them, do they? *Language in Society* 4: 289–94.

Du Bois, J. W., Schuetze-Cobun, S., Paolino, D. and Cumming, S. (1993) Outline of discourse transcription. In J. A. Edwards and M. D. Lampert (eds) *Talking Data: Transcription and Coding Methods for Language Research* 45–89. Hillsdale, NJ: Lawrence Erlbaum.

Edelsky, C. (1981) Who's got the floor? *Language in Society* 10: 383–421.

Edwards, E. R. (1903) *Etude Phonetique de la Langue Japonaise*. Leipzig : Impr. B. G. Teubner. 79.

Edwards, E. R. (1969) *Nihongo no Onseigakuteki Kenkyu (Studies of Japanese Phonetics)*. Tokyo: Kosesha Kosekaku.

Ekman, P. (1972) Universals and cultural differences in facial expressions of emotion. In J. Cole (ed.) *Nebraska Symposium of Motivation* 19. Lincoln, NE: University of Nebraska Press.

Ekman, P. (1973) *Darwin and Facial Expression: A Century of Research in Review*. New York: Academic Press.

Ekman, P. and Friesen, W. V. (1969) The repertoire of nonverbal behavior: categories, origins, usage, and coding. *Semiotica* 1: 49–98.

Ekman, P. and Friesen, W. V. (1971) Constants across cultures in the face and emotion. *Journal of Personality and Social Psychology* 17, 124–9.

Ekman, P, Friesen, W.V., O'Sullivan, M., Chan, A., Diacoyanni-Tarlatzis, I., Heider, K., Krause, R., LeCompte, W. A., Pitcairn, T., and Ricci-Bitti, P. E. (1987) Universals and cultural differences in the judgments of facial expressions of emotions. *Journal of Personality and Social Psychology* 53(4): 712–17.

Ellis, H. (1929) *Man and Woman*. Boston, MA: Houghton Mifflin. 103–4.

Etiquette for Ladies, with Hints on the Preservation, Improvement, and Display of *Female Beauty*. (1838) (1841) Philadelphia, PA: Carey, Lea & Blanchard.

Fairbanks, G. (1940) Recent experimental investigations of vocal pitch in speech. *Journal of Acoustical Society of America* 11: 457–66.

Fitch, J. L. and Holbrook, A. (1970) Modal fundamental frequency of young adults. *Archives of Otolaryngology* 92: 379–82.

Friesen, W. V. (1972) *Cultural Differences in Facial Expression in a Social Situation: An Experimental Test of The Concept of Display Rules*. Unpublished doctoral dissertation. University of California, San Francisco.

Fry, D. B. (1958) Experiments in the perception of stress. *Language and Speech* 1: 126–52.

Furo, H., 1996. Linguistic conflict of Japanese women: is that a request or an order? In N. Warner, J. Ahlers, L., Bilmes, M., Oliver, S., Wertheim, M., Chen (Eds), *Gender* and Belief Systems: Proceedings of the 4th Berkeley Women and Language Conference 247–59.

Gilbert, H. R. and Weismer, G. G. (1974) The effects of smoking on the speaking fundamental frequency of adult women. *Journal of Psycholinguistic Research* 3(3): 225–31.

Glasberg B. R. and Moore, B. C. J. (1990) Derivation of auditory filter shapes from notched-noise data. *Hearing Research* 47:103–38.

Goffman, E. (1967) *Interaction Ritual: Essays on Face to Face Behavior.* New York: Garden City.

Graddol. D. (1986) Discourse specific pitch behaviour. In C. Johns-Lewis (ed.) *Intonation in Discourse* 221–37. Croom Helm: London.

Graddol, D. and Swann, J. (1983) Speaking fundamental frequency: some physical and social correlates. *Language and Speech* 26 (4): 351–66.

Graddol, D. and Swann, J. (1989) *Gender Voices.* Oxford: Basil Blackwell Ltd.

Greenwood, D. D. (1961) Critical bandwidth and the frequency coordinates of the basilar membrane. *Journal of Acoustical Society of America* 33: 1344–56.

Greenwood, D. D. (1990) A cochlear frequency-position function for several species –years later. *Journal of Acoustical Society of America* 87: 2592–605.

Gumperz, J. J. (1987) Preface. *Politeness: Some Universals in Language Usage. Studies in Interactional Sociolinguistics* 4: xii–xiv. Cambridge: Cambridge University Press.

Gunter, C. D. and Mannning, W. H. (1982) Listener estimations of speaker height and weight in unfiltered and filtered conditions. *Journal of Phonetics* 10: 251–7.

Halliday, M. A. K. (1967) *Intonation and Grammar in British English.* The Hague: Mouton.

Hanley, T. D. and Snidercor, J. C. (1967) Some acoustic similarities among languages. *Phonetica* 17: 141–8.

Hanley, T. D. Snidercor, J. C. and Ringel, R. (1966) Some acoustic differences among Languages. *Phonetica* 14: 97–107.

Henton, G. C. (1989) Fact and fiction in the description of female and male pitch. *Language and Communication* 9(4): 299–311.

Henton, G. C. (1995) Pitch dynamism in female and male speech. *Language and Communication* 15 (1): 43–61.

Henneke, B. G. and Dumit, E. S. (1959) *The Announcer's Handbook.* New York: Holt, Rinehart and Winston.

Hermes, D. J. and van Gestel, J. C. (1991) The frequency scale of speech intonation. *Journal of Acoustical Society of America* 90 (1): 97–102.

Higurashi, Y. (1983) *The Accent of Extended Word Structures in Tokyo Japanese.* Tokyo: Educa.

Hirano, M. (1983) The structure of the vocal folds. In K. Stevens and M. Hirano (eds) *Vocal Folds Physiology* 33–43. Tokyo: University of Tokyo.

Hirose, H. (1997) Investigating the physiology of laryngeal structures. In Hardcastle W. J. and Laver, J. (eds) *The Handbook of Phonetics Sciences* 116–136. Oxford: Blackwell Publishers.

Hofstede, G. (1980) *Culture's Consequences.* Beverly Hills, CA: Sage.

Hofstede, G. (1983) Dimensions of national cultures in fifty countries and three regions. In J. B. Deregowski, S. Dziuraweic, and R. C. Annis (eds) *Explications in Cross-cultural Psychology* 335–55. Lisse, The Netherlands: Swets and Zeitlinger.

Hofstede, G. (1994) *Cultures and Organizations-Intercultural Cooperation and Its Importance for Survival-Software of the Mind*. London: HarperCollins Publishers.

Hollien, H. (1960) Vocal pitch variation related to changes in vocal fold length. *Journal of Speech Language and Hearing Research* 3 (2): 150–6.

Hollien, H., Dew, D. and Philips, P. (1971) Phonational frequency ranges of adults. *Journal of Speech and Hearing* 14: 755–60.

Hollien, H. and Jackson, B. (1973) Normative data on the speaking fundamental frequency characteristics of young adult males. *Journal of Phonetics* 1: 117–20.

Hollien, H. and Paul, P. (1969) A second evaluation of the speaking fundamental frequency characteristics of post-adolescent girls. *Language and Speech* 12: 119–24.

Hollian, H. and Shipp, T. (1972) Speaking fundamental frequency and chronological age in males. *Journal of Speech and Hearing Research* 15: 155–9.

Holmes, J. (1990) Hedges and boosters in women's and men's speech. *Language and Communication* 10 (30): 185–205.

Holmes, J. (1993) New Zealand women are good to talk to: an analysis of politeness strategies in interaction. *Journal of Pragmatics* 20: 91–116.

Hombert, J. M. (1977) Consonant types, vowel quality, and tone. In V. Fromkin (ed.) *Tone: A Linguistic Survey* 77–111. New York: Academic.

Honjo, I. and Isshiki, N. (1980) Laryngoscopic and voice characteristics of aged persons. *Archives of Otolaryngology* 106: 149–50.

Howells, W. D. (1906). Our daily speech. *Harper's Bazaar*. 40: 930–4.

Hudson, A. I. and Holbrook, A. (1981) A study of the reading fundamental vocal frequency of young Black adults. *Journal of Speech and Hearing Research* 24: 197–201.

Huttar, G. (1968) Relations between prosodic variables and emotions in normal American English Utterances. *Journal of Speech and Hearing Research* 11: 467–80.

Ide, S. (1982) Japanese sociolinguistics: politeness and women's language. *Lingua* 57: 357–85.

Ide, S. (1989) Formal forms and discernment: two neglected aspects of universals of linguistic politeness. *Journal of Cross-cultural and Interlanguage Communication* 8 (2/3): 223–48.

Ide, S. (1991) How and why do women speak more politely in Japanese. In S. Ide and N. Hanaoka McGloin (eds) *Aspects of Japanese Women's Language*. Tokyo: Kuroshio Shuppan.

Ito, K. (1986) A basic study on voice sound involving emotion (III): Non-stationary analysis of single vowel [e]. *The Japanese Journal of Ergonomics* 211–17.

Izard, C. E. (1971) *The Face of Emotion*. New York: Appleton-Century-Crofts.

James, H. (1881) *The Portrait of a Lady*. Boulder, CO: Raleigh, N.C. Alex Catalogue. Retrieved from NetLibrary: http://www.netlibrary.com

James, W. (1884) What is an emotion? *Mind* 9: 188–205.

Jassem, W. (1971) Pitch and compass of the speaking voice. *Journal of International Phonetic Association* 1: 59–68.

Jespersen, O. (1922) *Language, Its Nature, Development, and Origin*. New York: Henry Holt.

Jimbo, K. (1925) The Word-tone of the standard Japanese language. *Bulletin of the School of Oriental Studies, University of London* 3(4): 659–67.

Johns-Lewis, C. M. (1986) Prosodic differentiation of discourse modes. In C. Johns-Lewis (ed.) *Intonation in Discourse* 199–219. San Diego, CA: College-Hill Press Inc.

Kagitcibasi, C. (1997) Individualism and collectivism. In J. W. Berry, M. H. Segall, and C. Kagitcibasi (eds) *Handbook of Cross-cultural Psychology 3: Social Behavior and Applications* 1–49. Boston, MA: Allyn and Bacon.

Kahane, J. (1978) A morphological study of the human prepubertal and pubertal larynx. *American Journal of Anatomy* 151, 11–20.

Kanetsune K. (1938) *Nippon no Kotoba to Uta no Kozo (Structure of Japanese Words and Songs)*. Tokyo: Iwanami Shoten.

Kasuya, H., Suzuki, H., and Kido, K. (1968) Changes in pitch and first three formant frequencies of five Japanese vowels with age and sex of speakers. *Nihon Onkyo Gakkaishi (Journal of Acoustical Society of Japan)* 24(6): 355–64.

Kawakami, S. (1977) *Nihongo Onsei Gaisetsu (Overview of Japanese Sound)*. Tokyo: Ofusha.

Kawabata, Y. (1956) *Snow Country*. Translated with an introduction by E. G. Seidensticker. New York: Alfred Knopf.

Key, M. R. (1972) Linguistic behavior of male and female. *Linguistics* 88: 15–31.

Kitahara, Y, Tohkura, Y. *et al.* (1989) Onsei no inritsu joho to kanjo hyogen (prosodic information of sound and expression of emotion). *The Technical Report of the Institute of Electronics Information and Communication Engineers of Japan* March: SP88–158.

Kitajima, K. (1973) An analysis of pitch perturbation in normal and pathologic voices. *Practica Otol* 66: 1195–213.

Klatt, D. H. (1972) Discrimination of fundamental frequency contours in synthetic speech: implications for models of pitch perception. *The Journal of Acoustical Society of America* 53(1): 8–16.

Koda, R. (1982) *Pagoda, Skull, and Samurai: Three Stories*. Translated by Chieko Irie Mulhern. Ithaca, NY: China-Japan Program, Cornell University.

Kramer, C. (1975a) Excessive loquacity: women's speech as presented in American etiquette books. *Proceedings of the Speech Communication Association's Summer Conference XI. Austin, Texas* 47–55.

Kramer, C. (1975b) Women's speech: separate but unequal? In B, Thorne and N. Henley (eds) *Language and Sex: Difference and Dominance* 205–309. Rowley, MA: Newbury House Publishers Inc.

Kristof, N. D. (1995) Japan's feminine falsetto falls right out of favor. *New York Times*, December 13.

Kawakami, S. (1977) *Nihongo Onsei Gaisetsu (Overview of Japanese Sound)*. Tokyo: Ofusha.

LaBarre, W. (1947) The cultural basis of emotions and gestures. *Journal of Personality* 16: 49–68.

LaBarre, W. (1962) Some observations on character structure in the Orient: The Japanese. In B. S. Silberman (ed.) *Japanese Character and Culture* 325–59. Tucson, AZ: University of Arizona Press.

Ladd, D. R. (1980) *The Structure of Intonational Meaning: Evidence from English*. Bloomington, IN: Indiana University Press.

Ladd. D. R. (1996) *Intonational Phonology*. Cambridge: Cambridge University Press.

Ladd, D. R. and Silverman, K. E. A. (1984) Vowel intrinsic pitch in connected speech. *Phonetica*. 41:31–40.

Ladd, D. R., Silverman, K. E. A., Tolkmitt, F., Bergmann, G., and Scherer, K. R. (1985) Evidence for the independent function of intonation contour type, voice quality, and f0 range in signaling speaker affect. *Journal of the Acoustical Society of America* 78(1): 435–44.

Ladefoged, P. (1982) *A Course in Phonetics*. Orlando, FL: Harcourt Brace Jovanovich, Inc.

Lakoff, R. (1973) The logic of politeness; or minding your p's and p's. *Proceedings of the Ninth Regional Meeting of the Chicago Linguistic Society* 292–305.

Lakoff, R. (1975) *Language and Women's Place*. New York: Harper and Row.

Lambrecht, K, (1996) *Information Structure and Sentence Form: Topic, Focus, and the Mental Representations of Discourse Referents (Cambridge Studies in Linguistics)*. Cambridge: Cambridge University Press.

Lange, C. G. and James, W. (1922) *The Emotions (Volume I)*. Baltimore, MD: Williams & Wilkins Co.

Lass, N. J. and Brown W. S. (1978) Correlational study of speakers' heights, weights, body surface areas, and speaking fundamental frequencies. *The Journal of Acoustical Society of America* 63(4), 1218–20.

Lass, N. J., Barry, A. S., Walsh, J. M., and Amuso, T. A. (1979) The effect of temporal speech alterations on the speaker height and weight identification. *Language and Speech* 22: 163–71.

Lass, N. J., Brong, G. W., Ciccolella, S. A., Walters, S. C., and Maxwell, E. L. (1980) An investigation of speaker height and weight discriminations by means of paired comparison judgments. *Journal of Phonetics* 8: 205–12.

Lebra, T. S. (1976) *Japanese Patterns of Behavior*. Honolulu, HI: University Press.

Lehiste, I. and Peterson, G. E. (1961) Some basic considerations in the analysis of intonation. *Journal of Acoustical Society of America* 33: 419–25.

Lieberman, P. (1967) *Intonation, Perception and Language*. Cambridge, MA: The MIT Press.

Linke, C. E. (1973) A study of pitch characteristics of female voices and their relationship to vocal effectiveness. *Folia Phoniatrica* 25: 173–85.

Loveday, L. (1981) Pitch, politeness and sexual role. *Language and Speech* 24(1): 71–89.

Luchsinger, R. and Arnold, G. E. (1965) *Voice, Speech, Language: Clinical Communicology: Its Physiology and Pathology.* Translated by G. E. Arnold, and E. R. Finkbeiner. Belmont: Wardworth Publishing Company, Inc. and Constable & Co. Ltd.

Maass, A., Milesid, A., Zabbini, S., and Stahlber, D. (1995) Linguistic intergroup bias: Differential expectancies or in-group protection? *Journal of Personality and Social Psychology* 57: 981–93.

Majewski, W., Hollien, H. and Zalewski, J. (1972) Speaking fundamental frequency of Polish adult males. *Phonetica* 25 (2): 119–25

Mannes, M. (1969) Women are equal but –. In J. M. Bachelor, R. L. Henry, and R. Salisbury (eds) *Current Thinking and Writing.* New York: Appleton-Century-Crofts.

Mashimo, S. (1949) *Fujingo no Kenkyu (Studies of Women's Language).* Tokyo: Toa Shuppan.

Mashimo, S. (1969) *Fujingo no Kenkyu (Studies of Women's Language).* Tokyo: Tokyodo Shuppan.

Masini. (1893) Laringoscopia di 50 prostitute. *Archivio di Psichiatria* XIV, Fasc. I-II: 145.

Matsumoto, D., and Ekman, P. (1989) American-Japanese cultural differences in judgments of facial expressions of emotion. *Motivation and Emotion* 13: 143–57.

Matsumoto, D. (1991) Cultural influences on facial expressions of emotion. *Southern Communication Journal.* 56: 128–37.

Matsumoto, D. (1996) *Unmasking Japan: Myths and Realities About the Emotions of the Japanese.* Stanford, CA: Stanford University Press.

Matsumoto, D., Kudoh, T. Scherer, K., and Wallbot, H. (1988) Antecedents of and reactions to emotions in the United States and Japan. *Journal of Cross Cultural Psychology* 19: 267–86.

Matsumoto, K. (1996) *Intonation Units in Conversational Japanese: Structure and Linkage.* University of California, Los Angeles. Unpublished Ph.D. dissertation.

Matsumoto, Y. (1998). Stylistic Choices in Japanese across generations. A paper presented at the First International Conference on Practical Linguistics of Japanese (San Francisco).

McCawley, J. D. (1968) *The Phonological Component of a Grammar of Japanese.* The Hague: Mouton.

MCawley, J. D. (1977) Accent in Japanese. In L. M. Hyman (ed.) *Studies in Stress and Accent (SCOPIL 4)* 261–302. Los Angeles, CA: University of Southern California Department of Linguistics.

McConnell-Ginet. S. (1978) Intonation in a men's world. *Signs: Journal of Women, Culture, and Society* 3(3): 541–59.

McGloin, N. H. (1991) Sex difference and sentence-final particles. In: S, Ide and N. H. McGloin (eds) *Aspects of Japanese Women's Language*. Tokyo: Kurosio Publishers.

McGlone, R. E. and Hollien, H. (1963). Voice pitch characteristics of aged women. *Journal of Speech and Hearing Research* 6: 167–72.

McIntosh, C. W., Jn. (1939) A study of the relationship between pitch variability in the voices of superior speakers. Ph.D. dissertation, University of Iowa.

Menoto no Soshi (Booklet for Nursemaids). (1911) *Nihon Kyoiku Bunko Jokun Hen*. 35

Michel, J. F., Hollien, H., and Moore, P. (1966). Speaking fundamental frequency characteristics of 15, 16, and 17 year-old girls. *Language and Speech*, 9, 46–51.

Miller, A. (1967) *The Japanese Language*. Chicago, IL: The University of Chicago Press.

Moore, B. C. J. (1997) *An Introduction to the Psychology of Hearing*. London: Academic Press.

Moore, B. C. J. and Glasberg, B. R. (1983) Suggested formulae for calculating auditory-filter band widths and excitation patterns. *Journal of Acoustical Society of America* 74(3): 750–3.

Muranaka, C. (1996) Women newscasters lowering pitch. *The Daily Yomiuri*, June 13.

Murasaki, S. (1960) *The Tale of Genji*. Translated by A. Waley. Modern Library.

Mysak, E. D. (1959) Pitch and duration characteristics of older males. *Journal of Speech and Hearing Research* 2: 46–54.

Namura, J. (1692) *Onna Chohoki (Records of Women's Important Treasure)*. Kyoto: Yoshinoya Jirobe.

Namura, J. 1981. *Nan Chohoki (Records of Men's Valuable Treasures)*. Kinsei Bungaku Shoshi Kenkyukai hen (Modern Literature Bibliography Society (ed.)). Tokyo: Benseisha (Photo reproduction of originally publication in 1693).

Natsume, S. (1968) *Botchan*. Translated by U. Saski. Rutland. VT.: C. E. Tuttle Co.

Nitobe, I. (1905) *Bushido: the Soul of Japan*. New York; London: G. P. Putnam's Sons.

Niwa S. (1970) Changes of voice characteristics in urgent situation I (Kinkyuji ni okeru onsei henyo no kenkyu 1). *Report of the Aeromedical Laboratory, Japan Air Self Defense Force (Koku igaku jikkentai hokoku)* 11(1): 51–8.

Niwa S. (1971) Changes of voice characteristics in urgent situation II ((Kinkyuji ni okeru onsei henyo no kenkyu 1I). *Report of the Aeromedical Laboratory, Japan Air Self Defense Force (Koku igaku jikkentai hokoku)* 11: 246–51

Nolan, F. (1983) *The Phonetic Bases of Speaker Recognition*. Cambridge: Cambridge University Press.

Nooteboom, S. (1997) The prosody of speech melody and rhythm. In W. J. Hardcastle and J. Laver (eds) *The Handbook of Phonetics Sciences*. Oxford: Blackwell Publishers.

Ohala. J. J. (1973) Explanations for the intrinsic pitch of vowels. *Monthly Internal Memorandum, Phonology Lab (University of California, Berkeley)* 12: 9–24.

Ohara, Y. (1992) Gender-dependent pitch levels: A comparative study in Japanese and English. *Locating Power: Proceedings of the Second Berkeley Women and Language Conference* 2: 469–77.

Ohara, Y. (1999) Performing gender through voice pitch: a cross-cultural analysis of Japanese American English. In U. Pasero and F. Braun (eds) *Wahrnehmung und Hersellung von Geschlecht: Perceiving and Performing Gender* 105–16. Opladen (Wiesbaden): Westdeutscher Verlag.

Okamoto, S. and Sato, S. (1992) Less feminine speech among young Japanese females. *Locating Power: Proceedings of the Second Berkeley Women and Language Conference.* 2: 478–88.

Olwen, H. E. (1978) Sex differences in speech style. *Women Speaking* 4: 4–8.

Patterson, R. D. (1976) Auditory filter shapes derived with noise stimuli. *Journal of Acoustical Society of America* 59(3): 640–54.

Perkell, J. (1997) Articulatory processes. In W. J. Hardcastle and J. Laver (eds) *The Handbook of Phonetics Sciences* 333–70. Oxford: Blackwell Publishers.

Petersen, N. R. (1976) Intrinsic fundamental frequency of Danish vowels. *Annual Report of Institute of* Phonetics (University of Copenhagen) 10:1–27.

Preisler, B. (1986) *Linguistic Sex Roles in Conversation.* New York: Mouton de Gruyter.

Pike, K. L. (1945) *The Intonation of American English.* Ann Arbor, MI: University of Michigan Publications.

Philhour, W. Jr. (1948) *An Experimental Study of the Relationships Between Perception of Vocal Pitch and Connected Speech and Certain Measures of Vocal Frequency.* Ph.D. dissertation. University of Iowa.

Pierrehumbert, J. and Beckman, M. (1988) *Japanese Tone Structure (Linguistic Inquiry Monograph 15).* Cambridge, MA: The MIT Press.

Plutchik. R. (1980) A general psychoevolutionary theory of emotion. In R. Plutchik and H. Kellerman (eds) *Emotion: Theory, Research, and Experience* 3–33. New York: Academic Press. Inc.

Plutchik. R. and Kellerman, H. (1980) Preface. In R. Plutchik and H. Kellerman (eds) *Emotion: Theory, Research, and Experience: Vol. 1. Theories of Emotion.* New York: Academic Press Inc.

Provonost, G. E. (1939) An experimental study of natural and habitual pitch levels of superior speakers. Ph.D. Dissertation. (State) University of Iowa.

Provonost, G. E. (1942) An experimental study of methods for determining natural and habitual pitch. *Speech Monographs* 9: 111–13.

Rietveld, A. C. M., and Gussenhoven, C. (1985) On the relation between pitch excursion size and prominence. *Journal of Phonetics* 13: 299–308.

Rossing, T. (1982) *The Science of Sound.* Reading, MA: Addison-Wesley Publishing Company, Inc.

Ruscher, J. B. and Fiske, S. T. (1990) Interpersonal competition can cause individuating processes. *Journal of Personality and Social Psychology* 58: 832–43.

Ruscher, J. B. and Hammer, E. D. (1994) Revising disrupted impressions through conversation. *Journal of Personality and Social Psychology* 66: 530–41.

Ryan, M. G. (1990) *Japan's First Modern Novel, Ukigumo of Futabatei Shimei*. Ann Arbor, MI: Center for Japanese Studies, University of Michigan.

Sakuraba, K., Imaizumi, S. and Kakehi, K. (2004) Emotional expression in "Picahuu". *The Journal of the Phonetic Society of Japan* 8 (1): 77–84.

Sattel, J. (1976) The expressive male: tragedy or sexual politics? *Social Problem* 23: 467–77.

Saxman, J. H. and Burke, K. W. (1967) Speaking fundamental frequency characteristics of middle-aged females. *Folia Phoniatrica* 19: 167–72.

Scherer, K. R. (1986b) Vocal affect expression: a review and a model for future research. *Psychological Bulletin* 99(2): 143–65.

Schachter, S and Singer, J. E. (1962) Cognitive, social and physiological determinants of emotional state. *Psychological Review* 69: 379–99.

Scherer, K. R., Banse, R. and Wallbott, H. G. (2001) Emotion inferences from vocal expression correlate across languages and cultures. *Journal of Cross-Cultural Psychology* 32(1): 76–92.

Scripture, E. W. (1902) *The Elements of Experimental Phonetics*. New York: Scribner and Sons.

Seidler, V. (1989) *Rediscovering Masculinity: Reason, Language and Sexuality*. London: Routledge.

Seward, J. (1968). *Japanese in Action: An Unorthodox Approach to the Spoken Language and the People Who Speak It*. New York and Tokyo: Walker/ Weatherhil.

Shadle, C. H. (1985) Intrinsic fundamental frequency of vowels in sentence context. *Journal of Acoustical Society of America* 78: 1562–7.

Skinner, E. R. A. (1935) A calibrated recording and analysis of the pitch, force and quality of vocal tones expressing happiness and sadness; and a determination of the pitch and force of the subjective concepts of ordinary, soft and loud tones. *Speech Monographs* 22: 81–137.

Smith, J. S. (1992) Politeness and directives in Japanese women's speech. *Language in Society* 21 (1): 59–82.

Snidercor, J. C. (1943) A comparative study of pitch and duration characteristics of impromptu speaking and oral reading. *Speech Monographs* 10: 50–6.

Snidercor, J. C. (1951) The pitch and duration characteristics of superior female speakers during oral reading. *Journal of Speech and Hearing Disorders* 15: 44–52.

Stoicheff, M. L. (1981) Speaking fundamental frequency of middle-aged females. *Folia Phoniatrica* 19: 167–72.

Sugihara Y. and Katsurada, E. (2000) Gender-role personality traits in Japanese culture. *Psychology of Women Quarterly* 24: 309–18. Cambridge: Cambridge University Press.

Sulter, A. M., Schutte, H. K. and Miller, D. G. (1996) Standardized laryngeal videostroboscopic rating: differences between untrained and trained male and female subjects, and effects of varying sound intensity, fundamental frequency and age. *The Journal of Voice* 10(2): 175–89.

Sunaoshi, Y. (1994) Mild directives work effectively: Japanese women in command. In M. Bucholtz, A. C., Liang, L. A., Sutton, C., Hines (eds), *Cultural Performances: Proceedings of the 3rd Berkeley Women and Language Conference* 678–690.

Sunaoshi, Y., 1995. Your boss is your 'mother': Japanese women's construction of an authoritative position in the workplace. *Texas Linguistic Forum*, 34 (Department of Linguistics, University of Texas at Austin) 175–88.

Taguchi, K. (1889) Archiv für anatomie und physiologie. *Physiologische Abteilung*. Heft 5–6.

Tajfel, H. (1982) Social psychologoy of intergroup relation. *Annual Review of Psychology* 33: 1–39.

Takano, S. (2005) Re-examining linguistic power: strategic uses of directives by professional Japanese women in positions of authority and leadership. *Journal of Pragmatics* 37: 633–66.

Takekuro, M. (2002) Indexicality and socialization: Age-graded changes of young Japanese women's speech. In K. Kataoka and S. Ide (eds.) *Bunka, Intaakushon, Gengo (Culture, Interaction, and Language)* 195–214. Tokyo: Hitsuji Shobo.

Terango. L. (1966) Pitch and duration characteristics of the oral reading of males on a masculinity-femininity dimension. *Journal of Speech and Hearing Research* 9: 590–5.

Terasawa, R., Kakita, Y., and Hirano, M. (1984) Simultaneous measurements of mean air flow rate, fundamental frequency and voice intensity: results from 30 normal male and 30 normal female subjects. *Onseigengoigaku (The Japan Journal of Logopedics and Phoniatrics)* 25: 189–207.

Teshigawara, M. (2004) Voice quality of the bad guys compared to those of the good guys. *The Journal of the Phonetic Society of Japan* 8 (1): 60–76.

Thorne, B. Kramarae, C, and Henley, N. (1983) Language, gender, and society: opening a second decade of research. In B. Thorne, C. Kramarae, and N. Henley (eds) *Language, Gender, and Society* 7–24. Boston, MA: Newbury House.

Titze, I. R. (1989). Physiologic and acoustic differences between male and female voices. *Journal of Acoustical Society of America* 85 (4): 1699–1707.

Trager, G. (1949) *The Field of Linguistics*. Norman, OK: Battenberg Press. 8.

Trager, G. L. (1958) Paralanguage: a first approximation. *Studies In Linguistics* 13: 1–12.

Tsuge, S., Kakami, K. Fukaya, M. (1987) Speakers' height, weight and voice pitch (1): on correlation of speakers height, weight, and pitch frequencies of Japanese five vowels. *Bulletin Phonetics Japan* 185: 2–5.

Twain, M. (1998) *The Adventures of Tom Sawyer (Oxford World's Classics)*. L. C. Mitchell (ed.) Oxford: Oxford University Press.

Ueda, A. (1974) *Ugetsu Monogatari (Tales of Moonlight and Rain)*. Translated and edited by Leon M. Zolbrod. Vancouver: University of British Columbia Press.

Uemura, G. (1910) Onna Chuyo (Women's Moderation). *Nihon Kyoiku Bunko 10 (Kyokasho Hen)*: 112–48.

Uldall, E. (1960) Attitudinal meanings conveyed by intonation contours. *Language and Speech* 3: 223–34.

Umeda, N. (1981) Influence of segmental factors on fundamental frequency in fluent speech. *The Journal of Acoustical Society of America.* 70: 350–5.

Utsuki, N., and Okamura, N. (1976) Relationship between emotional state and fundamental frequency of speech (Jodo to onsei kihon shuhasu no kankei ni tsuite). *Reports of the Aeromedical Laboratory, Japan Self-Defense Force (Koku Igaku Jikkentai Hokoku)* 16: 179–88.

Valentine, H. and Thompson, A. (1938) *Better Than Beauty: A Guide to Charm.* New York: Modern Age Books, Inc.

Van Bezooijen, R. (1995) Sociocultural aspects of pitch differences between Japanese and Dutch women. *Language and Speech* 38(3): 253–65.

Van Bezoonijen, R, Otto, S. A. and Heenan, T. A. (1983) Recognition of vocal expressions of emotion: A three-nation study to identify universal characteristics. *Journal of Cross-Cultural Psychology* 14: 387–406.

Vance, T. J. (1986) The monotony of Japanese intonation. 197th Meeting of the American Oriental Society.

Weaver, A. T. (1924) Experimental studies in vocal expression. *Journal of Applied Psychology* 1: 23–51.

Wells, R. A. (1800) *Manners, Culture and Dress of the Best American Society.* King MA and IA): Richardson & Co., Publisher.

Woods, N. (1992) It's not what she says, it's the way she says it: the influence of speaker-sex on pitch and intonation patterns. Paper presented at the Workshop on Prosody in Natural Speech Data at the University of Pennsylvania. 5–12.

Yamazawa, H. (1987) Speaking fundamental frequency characteristics of Japanese females: unpublished pilot study.

Yamazawa, H. and Hollien, H. (1992) Speaking fundamental frequency patterns of Japanese women. *Phonetica* 49: 128–40.

Yamamoto, T. (1979) *Hagakure (The Book of the Samurai)* Translated by W. S. Wilson. Kondansha International Ltd.

Yuasa, I. (1998) Politeness strategies observed in pitch-ranges employed by Japanese men and women. *Crossroads of Language, Interaction, and Culture* I: 27-42. Los Angeles, CA: the Regents of the University of California.

Yuasa, I. (1999) Effects of interlocutors' gender on pitch-ranges employed by Japanese Men. *The Proceedings of the 14th International Congress of Phonetic Sciences* 2: 1605–8.

Yuasa, I. (2001) *Politeness, Emotion, and Gender: A Sociophonetic Study of Voice Pitch Modulation.* Ph.D. Dissertation. University of California, Berkeley.

Yuasa, I. P. (2002) Empiricism and emotion: representing and interpreting pitch ranges. In S. Benor, M. Rose, D. Sharma, J. Sweetland, and Q. Zhang (eds) *Gendered Practices in Language* 193-209. Stanford, CA: CSLI Publications.

Yuasa, I. P. (2003) Socio-cultural usage of creaky voice: Creaky voice of American and Japanese women, The 15th International Congress of Phonetic Sciences (Barcelona, Spain).

Yuasa, I. P. (2006). A cross-cultural, gender-based comparison of creaky voice usage between Americans and the Japanese. The Joint Conference of AAAL(American Association for Applied Linguistics) and ACLA/CAAL (Canadian Association of Applied Linguistics) (Montreal, Canada).

Yuasa, I. P. (2007). A cross-cultural, gender-based comparison of creaky voice usage between Americans and the Japanese: A Perception Study. The 2007 ATJ (the Association of Teachers of Japanese) Seminar (Boston).

Zee, E. (1978) The interaction of tone and vowel quality. *UCLA Working Papers in Phonetics* 41: 53–67.

CPSIA information can be obtained
at www.ICGtesting.com
Printed in the USA
JSHW020545160520
5718JS00002B/6

9 781845 539061